Notes on the Holiness of God

Notes on the Holiness of God

David Willis

WILLIAM B. EERDMANS PUBLISHING COMPANY
GRAND RAPIDS, MICHIGAN / CAMBRIDGE, U.K.

Wm. B. Eerdmans Publishing Co.
255 Jefferson Ave. S.E., Grand Rapids, Michigan 49503 /
P.O. Box 163, Cambridge CB3 9PU U.K.

Printed in the United States of America

07 06 05 04 03 02   7 6 5 4 3 2 1

Library of Congress Cataloging-in-Publication Data

Willis, David (E. David)
Notes on the holiness of God / David Willis.
p.   cm.
Includes bibliographical references and index.
ISBN 0-8028-4987-3 (pbk.: alk. paper)
I. God — Holiness.   I. Title.

BT147.W55   2002
231′.4 — dc21
                                            2002072192

www.eerdmans.com

To

Ann Chandler Willis

Contents

Introduction

"You could be laying the holy table for mass the way you set those cuttings out. That's the deep truth of things too no matter or not if you know it." Ita's eyes disappeared entirely when she smiled. "Smirchy and holy is all one, my dear," she said. "I doubt Jarlath has taught you that. Monks think holiness is monkishness only. But somewheres you've learned the truth anyhow. You can squeeze into Heaven reeking of pig blood as well as clad in the whitest fair linen in the land."[1]

When it comes today to speaking of the holiness of God, there is a widespread confusion resulting from a compound mistake. The first part of the mistake is the tendency to treat transcendence and immanence as opposites (or worse, to speak of the transcendent God versus the immanent God). The second part of the mistake is the tendency still to think of transcendence and immanence as primarily spatial categories. The third part is the tendency to subsume holiness almost exclusively under God's transcendence.

1. Frederick Buechner, *Brendan* (New York: Atheneum, 1987), pp. 34-35.

I

This widespread confusion requires a compound correction. The first part of the correction is the recognition that, when used theologically, both transcendence and immanence refer to the living Subject who is present but also not restricted to that presence: the Holy One is present with but not bounded by the conditions of being present. The second part is the recognition that the separateness implied in the root meanings of "holy" refers primarily to uniqueness, not distance from. The third part is the recognition that holiness is a communicable perfection of God: creatures belonging to the Holy One grow in creaturely holiness, so that the *communio sanctorum* is more than a nominal reality.

The subject of this essay is the single transcending presence who is the living God.

Properly speaking, holiness is that pure love who is God eternally. This pure love is in every way prior to, is in every way the presupposition of, God's purifying love manifest in creaturely, derivative holiness. It is through the presence of the transcending one, especially in the cross of the risen and coming-again Jesus Christ, that God is known in the unequal reciprocity of divine and creaturely love, in the gracious freedom of initiative and response between uncreated and created love. That pure love is immediate to God eternally and, as purifying love, is mediate temporally, spatially, energetically to constitute creation and redemption.

Those who would undertake the critical examination of the doctrine of God's holiness are well advised to keep ever before them the experience of those who, with the best of intentions, rushed forward to keep the ark of the Lord from toppling over. People are not left unscathed when dealt with by the Holy One who is eternally Subject. This is not, as it is often taken to be, because God is punitively protective of the uniquely divine glory, somehow identified apart from a theology of the cross. The risk is because the pure and purifying love of God will not ultimately be thwarted no matter what. One does not remain unmarked by the costly love of the Holy One. But more of that in chapters 4, on purifying love, and 5, on the holiness of beauty.

To say that the subject of this study is immense is not a standard academic disclaimer about the laughably obvious. It is a scientific statement commensurate with the nature of the subject being studied. If by science one restricts oneself to empirically measurable knowledge and duplicable experiment, then statements used in the study of God are not scientific. If, however, by a science one means consequential search according to a method which is congruent with the subject being studied, then attention to holiness belongs to the discipline of critically examining the faith of the church, that is, belongs to systematic, or constructive, theology.

When I refer, as I just have, to the faith of the church, I have necessarily said something about the identity of the God whose holiness is to be studied. The reference implies what needs now, also at the outset, to be made explicit. Here God means the Holy Other One, the center of whose self-disclosure is Jesus Christ as witnessed to by the power of the Holy Spirit in the scriptures of the Old and New Testaments. The first chapter of this study, therefore, seeks to clarify what I mean when I refer to a theology of the cross. I mean a theology based on that particular cross on which Jesus Christ, the eternal Word made flesh and the same as the risen and coming-again Lord, was killed. The subsequent chapters are on different facets of this fundamental teaching.

I am working with the assumption that conduct, reflection, and speech about the living God are essentially doxological responses to God's Word to us. This self-disclosing Subject strikes us diversely according to the divine accommodation to our condition. It is only through this diverse accommodation that we experience the unity of the encountering Subject, and it is only because God freely chooses to be the referent of our analogical language that it becomes accurately *theo*logical. The plethora of literary styles, of analogies, of emotions, of aesthetic expressions, and of narrative accounts are invaluable parts of the church's proclamation and teaching. Confessional summaries of what is proper to God — the attributes or perfections of God — are not intended to be exhaustive; they are intended to hold together dialectically true and necessarily complementary affirmations.

There appear to be seasons (in Tillich's terms, the *kairoi* which symbols successively have) when this or that attribute is insufficiently attended to by individual theologians (who themselves are often making a necessary correction in another direction). The church's doctrine of God develops when a relatively neglected or misunderstood divine perfection is clarified, redefined, and given greater prominence. This development is the unfolding harmony — to use an older and more lively term than "systematic cohesion" — of dialectically maintained "evangelical truths" (to use the Barmen Declaration's term) whose Subject is the one Word of God which the true church hears, trusts, and obeys in life and in death. Such development today includes clarifying the meaning of the holiness of God and giving it a prominence which reorders the way the divine perfections are treated.

This essay began with a study of the doctrine of God according to the Reformed heritage. My research led me more firmly than ever to conclude that there is no single distinctive Reformed doctrine of God. The last thing Reformed theologians have wanted is to teach something other than the catholic doctrine of the Trinity as developed in the debates of the fourth and fifth centuries and formulated in the decisions of the first four ecumenical councils. There seem to be, however, certain ways the formally catholic doctrine of the Trinity functions which are perhaps more characteristic of the Reformed tradition than of other traditions. Thus the Reformed tradition may give proportionately greater attention than other traditions to the implications of the doctrine of the Trinity for such matters as: the relation between biblical language and more consciously philosophical language, the continuity between the Old and New Testaments, the criteria for distinguishing the living God from idols, and a this-worldly exercise of Christian piety.

I became intrigued with a particular instance which tells us a great deal about Reformed understandings of God, namely, interpretations of the second commandment by French Reformed theologians up to 1562 and their accompanying iconoclastic practices. Those practices sometimes led and sometimes followed doctrine. There were occasions in that polemical context when some Reformed theologians spoke as if iconoclasm belonged to the very nature of Christian piety and doctrine. That would be because — according to them — the God truly worshiped and obeyed is not merely invisible but essentially ineffable, not simply incomprehensible but essentially unimaginable. That is to say,

4

not only is God incapable of being grasped by the finite, but what we mean by God is that which is essentially ungraspable. Such teachings may be polemical exaggerations of necessary aspects of apophatic theology and the *via negativa,* but if pushed too far these exaggerations could suggest that unknowability is one of the divine attributes or perfections. That may be the direction some Reformed theologians moved during the decade of hardening of denominational lines in France, which hardening is tragically evident in the 1572 Saint Bartholomew's Day massacre. The presence of other voices, including those of irenic Roman Catholics and irenic Lutherans as well as more nuanced readers of Calvin, in this decade is not as well remembered as the extreme positions. Those less well-known voices deserve a hearing if we are to have a more accurate spectrum of Reformed understanding of God. I am continuing that research, and thereby intend to maintain the necessary connections among what are, disastrously to each, too often torn apart: systematic theology, history of doctrine, theological ethics, and aesthetics.

Aesthetics is not an appendage to other, supposedly "more serious" modes of the theological task, though one could easily get the impression that the subject comes up only as an afterthought or — worse — as a reservoir of useful illustrations of what can supposedly be thought and said better otherwise. Of course, there are those, like von Balthasar and Barth — to mention only two but most telling examples — who seriously and joyfully deal with the facts of beauty and its opposite as integral to ethics, systematics, and the history of doctrine. Practically the whole of Eastern Orthodoxy would approach holiness iconographically, icons being integral to every other dimension of Christian life.

At the outset, in this introduction, I need to state at least my intention if not my accomplishment: to recognize and make appropriate use of theopoiesis as often the most accurate, most precise, and fullest way of reflection on doctrine, in this case the doctrine of the divine attribute of holiness. I have been much influenced in this regard by the small volume by Amos Wilder with that title *(Theopoetic).* I do not mean that one gets something straight — let us say, rationally, consequentially, "logically" — only then to express the same in poetic categories. I just put "logically" in inverted commas because I recognize that there are forms of logic which while not being irrational, go beyond the rational, and there are even, as far as that goes, reasons of the heart which may often be more reliably clear than cogitation. I mean rather that the only revelation which comes to us efficaciously (else it is not revelation to us) is, often as not, in aesthetical categories. A method which is congruent with the subject will, in the case of holiness, attend to the ways reality is pointed to theopoetically. Besides, James Muilenburg was quite correct when he observed: "More than any others of our age, it is the poets, dramatists, and tellers of stories who penetrate most deeply into the mind and heart of contemporary man. They have declined the office of spectator, but have chosen instead to bring us to the place where words are spoken and heard, and thus to engage us in that interior conversation where the walls of our isolation and self-centeredness are broken down."[2]

I am aware that my meaning is from time to time best served with a somewhat new vocabulary. That new vocabulary in almost every instance is a recovery of a more seasoned, aged-in-oak parlance; at least I hope it is not entirely devoid of theopoiesis. When it comes to style, I am aware of several things: that frequently the sonorous memory of the liturgy has been known to drown out competing noises; that the fresh, delight-filled, unsentimental eloquence of children is often a subtext; that occasionally some useful colloquialisms, not unknown to Luther, have survived the dictates of more sniffy tastes; that Barth's syntax often, and felicitously, obtrudes; that Aquinas's way of setting key questions is usually quite patent; and that Calvin's preference for moderation and for the order of teaching has not been utterly ignored.

I am indebted to an innumerable, overlapping, ancient and modern multitude of family members, friends, fellow students, esteemed adversaries, authors, artists, musicians, and the beloved scruffy everywhere to whom we are blessed to belong. Having said that these influences,

2. James Muilenburg, *The Way of Israel: Biblical Faith and Ethics* (New York: Harper and Row, 1961), p. 13. Cf. Muilenburg's article "Holiness," in *The Interpreter's Dictionary of the Bible,* ed. George A. Buttrick et al., vol. 2 (Nashville: Abingdon, 1962).

only some of whom one may be aware of at a given season, are too numerous to mention, one would be ill advised to begin a detailed list of them. I do need, however, to acknowledge: the balance and clarity brought to the discussion of immanence and transcendence by William Placher; the visions of discipleship provided by Esther de Waal's works on Celtic and Benedictine (especially Cistercian) spirituality; Paul Lehmann's characteristic wedding of political conscience and theological dynamic; Roy Fairchild's fleshing out of the correlations between psychological and theological resources; James Loder's engagement in the interaction of theologically scientific and naturally scientific discourses; and Alexander McKelway's stubbornness for theological honesty and prophetic critique, savingly mixed with the necessary sense of irony. Father Georges Florovsky has had an influence on me in ways I am only still discovering, ways which go far beyond the formal content and discussions of his patristic seminars.

I want also at the very least to acknowledge my indebtedness to three resources of confrontation, guidance, pathos, and delight. The first is comprised of fellow participants in the international dialogues between the Reformed and the Russian Orthodox, between the Reformed and the Vatican, and among the World Council of Churches' erstwhile forums on other bilaterals. The second is comprised of colleagues — maintenance crews, faculty, administrators, trustees, librarians, students — in the communities of Princeton Theological Seminary; of San Francisco Theological Seminary and the Graduate Theological Union, Berkeley; of an earlier Harvard Divinity School; of the Reformed faculties of theology of Budapest and Debrecen; of the Presbyterian Seminary at Seoul; and of the Protestant continuing education consortium in Yangong. The Center of Theological Inquiry, Princeton, provided an invaluable context for discussing, rethinking, and reformulating many aspects of this topic. The third is comprised of those several persons into whose skilled hands earlier versions of this study fell. They thereby share the responsibility for what may prove to be useful, but they do not do so for what may not.

DAVID WILLIS
Princeton, New Jersey

CHAPTER ONE

The Holiness of the Cross

While every true doctrine is shaped by the theology of the cross, nowhere is a speculative theology more a temptation than with the doctrine of God. This is especially the case when it comes to thought and discourse about the divine attributes or perfections.[1] The theology of

---

1. For examples and selected texts of how the attributes of God's love, God's holiness, and God's righteousness were diversely treated by Reformed orthodox theologians, see Heinrich Heppe, *Reformed Dogmatics* (Grand Rapids: Baker, 1978), and Heinrich Heppe, *Die Dogmatik der evangelisch-reformierten Kirche,* ed. Ernst Bizer (Neukirchen: Buchhandlung des Erziehungsvereins, 1935), locus 5, sec. 29–34.1. The ordering of the loci in Heppe's *Reformed Dogmatics* could well foster the impression that one establishes first (actually after the questions of natural and revealed theology [locus 1] and the authority of Scripture [loci 2 and 3]) God's existence (locus 4) and God's attributes (locus 5) before the triune nature of God (locus 6), and well before treating the person and work of Christ (loci 17, 18, and 19). This arrangement is quite different from one which would reflect the conviction that the person and work of Christ (a) identify what we mean by God and (b) control our understanding of God's very being as triunely relational. Cf. Eberhard Jüngel, *God as the Mystery of the World* (Grand Rapids: Eerdmans, 1983), p. 13, cited in William Placher, "The Vulnerability of God," in *Toward the Future of Reformed Theology,* ed. D. Willis and M. Welker (Grand Rapids: Eerdmans, 1999), p. 202: "The Crucified One is virtually the real definition of what is meant with the word God." This is very much in keeping with Luther's dictum that "I neither have nor know any other God than that flesh which gestated in the womb of the Virgin Mary."

the cross restrains the kind of abstract guessing which the sixteenth-century French Christian humanists called "theologastry"; but it does much more than that. It frees the church to concentrate on the right material of sane doxology.

In this chapter we will consider, first, the use and abuse of a theology of the cross; second, the particular cross in question; and third, the identity of the person thereon crucified.

Cruciform Knowledge

Here the question is whether sane doctrine — wholesome teaching — concerning the holiness of God must begin with the cross. The question is begged by either a flat yes or no, leaving the terms in which it is asked unexamined. The first four chapters of 2 Corinthians constitute one of the classic passages which clarifies the question and re-poses it in different terms.

The immediate context is Paul's telling the congregation that he cannot come visit them after all, but that does not mean that God's purpose for them is sometimes yes and sometimes no. With God it is always yes. They are not to doubt their special place in God's purposes. In fact, those who put their trust in Jesus Christ are more evidently reflectors of God's likeness than even Moses. Paul dares to draw a comparison between, on the one hand, the former and passing ministry through Moses and the code written on stone, and, on the other hand, the new covenant according to which Paul assures the congregation at Corinth that they are a letter from Christ written with the Spirit not on stone but on the heart (2 Cor. 3:3-6). "Now if the dispensation of death, carved in letters on stone, came with such splendor [or glory] that the Israelites could not look at Moses' face because of its brightness, will not the splendor of the dispensation of the Spirit be all the greater?" (3:7-8).

An unveiling is entailed in this new covenant. This removal of the veil is the work of the Spirit, and seems to be equated in this passage by Paul with freedom. The unveiling means that while Moses' face was changed just by a glimpse of God's backside, and while even the splendor of the old ministry was so great that a veil was required, now, with the new covenant, with unveiled face we behold the glory of the Lord in such a way that we are being changed from one degree of glory to another: "Now the Lord is the Spirit, and where the Spirit is, there is freedom. And we all, with unveiled face, reflecting [or beholding] the glory of the Lord, are being changed into his likeness from one degree of glory to another; for this comes from the Lord who is the Spirit. Therefore, having this ministry as we have received mercy, we do not lose heart" (3:17–4:1).

The particularity of this unveiling is Christ. The minds of unbelievers remain darkened,[2] which keeps them from "seeing the light of the gospel of the glory of Christ, who is the likeness of God. For what we preach is not ourselves, but Jesus Christ as Lord, with ourselves as your servants for Jesus' sake. For it is the God who said, 'Let light shine out of darkness,' who has shone in our hearts to give the light of the knowledge of the glory of God in the face of Christ" (4:4-6 RSV).

Should anyone doubt the manifold meanings of any given passage of Scripture, he or she need only reread these opulent first four chapters of 2 Corinthians. Among those meanings there are three points worth noting which bear directly on the question before us.

First, "all the greater" in 3:8 is a way of comparing two realities such as law and gospel and old and new creation. This same mode of comparison also appears in the use of "more abounds" terms. For example, the

---

2. Hence the great attention given by the Cappadocians to true knowledge as entailing the healing and reilluminating of the mind. According to them, the eternal Logos, by whom all *logikoi* were made, comes and undarkens — releases from the power of darkness — by shining into the world. Otherwise the fallen *logikoi* would remain in the dark. In this teaching these Church Fathers are only expanding on a major theme in the Johannine literature, beginning with the prologue to John's Gospel and including the bald statement equating the right knowledge of God with life eternal. On this, cf. also Flannery O'Connor's *Wise Blood* for an accurate treatment of the seeing that is blind and the blindness that is seeing. The image of the light is so strong that it is one of the few chosen to be in the starkly succinct Nicene Creed: "And in one Lord, Jesus Christ, the only begotten Son of the Father, God of God, Light of Light, true God of true God, begotten not made, being of one substance with the Father, who for us and our salvation, came down. . . ."

strong word that "superabounds" or "abounds all the more" or "goes beyond the bounds" is the controlling form of comparison in Romans 5:20-21: "Law came in, to increase the trespass; but where sin increased, grace abounded all the more, so that, as sin reigned in death, grace also might reign through righteousness to eternal life through Jesus Christ our Lord" (RSV).[3]

Second, it is the same God who spoke in the beginning to create light who also shines forth in the face of Christ. God's work of redemption and God's work of creation are so held together as to be only mutually intelligible, complementarily experienced and defined. The narrative of God's faithful movement from old to new covenant is *mirrored* in the way believers, "reflecting [or beholding] the glory of the Lord, are being changed into his likeness from one degree of glory to another": the *procedure* of reflecting God's glory. This personal and social transformation is a sign of the continuing identity of the same God who deals with humans in the old dispensation and in the new covenant.

Third, much of Paul's argument in these chapters turns on the use made of "glory," the glory that was there in the old dispensation and the glory of the new covenant. Rather than there being a denigration of glory, or a setting of glory over against the cross, the cross redefines glory. God's dealing now through Christ and in the Spirit is far greater and more revealed — unveiled — than ever before. The new covenant is in Christ's body and blood; we are to preach Christ and him crucified; being a new creature in Christ entails cosuffering with coglorification.

Now, what of the question as posed in the beginning of this section? If we are to follow the lead of Paul, then we must confess that, yes, sane doctrine begins with the cross. However, two qualifications are necessary to clarify the contents of this affirmation.

The first qualification notes that there are at least two senses of beginning with the cross. One is to start with the cross at point A and

---

3. Jesus' teachings are rife with this mode of comparison, for example, when he compares the commandments as received and interpreted by the Pharisees and the commandments retaught by Jesus: "You have heard it said . . . but I say. . . ." Do men put new wine into old wineskins? "Unless your righteousness exceed that of the Pharisees. . . ."

move from there to point B and so on. The other sense is to start and stick with the cross at every point or locus. When we say that sane doctrine concerning the holiness of God begins with the cross, we mean it in the second sense. The *"archē"* in Origen's work, or what has survived of it, has this sense: *Peri Archōn* is concerning first things or basic realities or inevitably foundational matters which influence the content of every theological development. These first things are not chronological, or logical, starting blocks one gets out of and leaves behind to run a race and (in semi-Pelagian twang) "get on with the real business of doing theology." Development means unfolding the implications of something so that a new understanding of this or that topic emerges. Sane doctrine thinks and says more than that God is known and is redemptive through the cross, but it does not say or think anything less. Sane doctrine does not say or think through anything apart from the cross *(cruce remoto)*.[4] The cross, so to speak, is a crucial criterion by which doctrine at every point is put to the test.

The second qualification notes that there are now so many senses of "theology of the cross" that the term may have become an umbrella under which quite different theological positions and procedures commonly escape the glare of semantic discrimination. At least — and this is already a matter for rejoicing — almost everyone gathered under that umbrella knows that the cross is somehow central to his or her theology and ethics. At least almost everyone gathered there still sees, hears, smells, feels, tastes the scandal of combining "God" and "cross" to make a noun, "theology of the cross." It is not my lot here to disentangle the various understandings of the term, partly because it is a symbol whose breadth quickens many imaginations, an imaginative range which probably in the long run serves the diversity of contexts in which the gospel

---

4. In the apologetic aspect of Anselm's work, which he says he is doing for the moment *Christo remoto*, Christ is in fact never left aside. Anselm's *Christo remoto* is not unlike Bonhoeffer's *si Deus non daretur* and Calvin's *si stetisset Adam*. These considerations of *hypothetical* possibilities are sometimes used for catechetical purposes, but more often for seriously examining counterarguments which have weight and which force themselves on critical thinkers — which examination is, of course, eminently instructive.

is freshly proclaimed.[5] My lot is rather a more modest one of saying as clearly as I can what I mean by the term when I say sound doctrine begins with the cross and its interpretations.

What I mean by the theology of the cross is thought, praise, and behavior toward God which are continually shaped by focusing on the whole course of Christ's obedience unto the death on that particular cross whose saving power is vindicated by the resurrection and experienced by those who live in the sure hope of Christ's coming again.[6] In other words, it is theology which recognizes the epistemological priority of the *status humilitationis,* and which presupposes the ontological priority of the *status exaltationis* as the source and goal of Christ's saving person and work.[7]

The theology of the cross thus understood has a primary and a secondary function.

The primary function is antireductive and antidisjunctive. The theology of the cross thus understood functions to retain and hold together those parts of redemption which the Scriptures do not allow to be separated: incarnation, cross, resurrection, anointing of the many with the Spirit, ascension, and coming again to judge the living and the dead.

---

5. On the potential for abuse of a misunderstanding of a theology of the cross, without the resurrection specification of which cross, we can note Orlando Peterson's *Rituals of Blood;* but the latter's characterizing of Paul's theology of the cross as fanaticism is extreme — as is well noted and countered in Josiah U. Young's paper "Sharing God's Suffering at the Hands of a Godless World: Bonhoeffer's Path to the Triune God," read at the conference on "Christ the Center: The Legacy of Barth and Bonhoeffer for Today," Luther Seminary, Saint Paul, Minn., 24-26 July 2000.

6. Besides those studies noted in the *Evangelisches Kirchenlexikon*'s article "Theologia Crucis," see Gerhardt Forde's section on "Luther's Theology of the Cross," in *Christian Dogmatics,* ed. C. Braaten and R. Jenson, vol. 1 (Philadelphia: Fortress, 1984), pp. 47-63.

7. For a concise, solid summary of the main points of the Reformed emphases in understanding the person and work of Christ, see again chapter 5 of Jacques de Senarclens, *Heirs of the Reformation* (Philadelphia: Westminster, 1963), esp. pp. 211-29. See also Leanne Van Dyk, "Toward a New Typology of Reformed Doctrines of Atonement," in *Toward the Future of Reformed Theology,* ed. D. Willis and M. Welker (Grand Rapids: Eerdmans, 1999), pp. 225-38.

This function is especially called for in the face of the proliferation of genitive theologies: theology of this or that done, however, in such a piecemeal fashion that the congruence and interrelatedness of the body of Christian theology is neglected or denigrated. Holding together both states, humiliation and exaltation,[8] doing justice to both states in the mutuality of their definitions, is the opposite of an imposed contrariness between a so-called theology (or Christology) from below and a so-called theology (or Christology) from above. That is one of the points of the truth of the incarnation: the person and work of Christ are the uniting of those two movements, the inseparable and unconfused personal unity of these vectors.[9]

The theology of the cross thus understood functions secondarily as a prophetic protest against the false glory of abstraction, against the pseudopower of "freedom" from the Word of God in all his concreteness, locatedness, temporality, humanity. It functions to expose choosing pomp over poverty, choosing personal glorification over compassion, choosing the presence of the Messiah minus the labor of Mary, choosing the sages' visitation minus the dung of a manger, choosing the triumphal procession minus the cock's third crow, choosing forgiveness minus repentance — and choosing "Christ" minus the church (or, for that matter, choosing the "church" minus Christ), a matter to which we will return in chapter 2 on the *communio sanctorum*.

8. On the status of self-emptying and the status of exaltation treated as embodying God's covenanting fidelity, see Senarclens, pp. 234-40. See also Carl Braaten, "The Person of Jesus Christ," in *Christian Dogmatics*, 1:465-543, esp. sec. 6, pp. 545-56. The states of Christ's self-emptying and exaltation are the subject of locus 18 of Heppe's *Reformed Dogmatics*.

9. Other movements are united there, such as: the present movement from future to past and past to future; the movement from possibility to actuality; the movement forward and laterally; the movement which goes beyond the four dimensions. Put otherwise, the one-person unity of God and man *(ho theanthrōpos hagios)* judges as speculatively abstract both (a) a so-called theology from below which defines itself as the opposite of a purely from-above theology (if indeed there is actually such a thing except in polemical strategy) and (b) a so-called theology from above which defines itself as the opposite of a purely from-below theology (if indeed there is actually such a thing except in polemical strategy).

The Cross of the Risen Lord

Here the question is whether the person who suffered death on that particular cross is the same one whom the disciples recognized as the risen Jesus Christ.

In the earliest apostolic preaching and onward, the answer to that question is straightforward: Yes. Yes, the crucified, dead, and buried Jesus of Nazareth is the same person who has been raised from the dead and who has appeared to chosen witnesses. The cross in the theology of the cross is confessed to be saving because of the vindication of Jesus as the prophesied Messiah by his being raised from the dead and by his sending of the promised Spirit in these last times. On the Day of Pentecost Peter proclaims, "This Jesus God raised up, of which we are witnesses. Thus, being exalted to the right hand of God and receiving from the Father the promised Holy Spirit, he spread out this which you now see and hear" (Acts 2:32-33).

This defines the particular cross among many crosses. The cross that examines every theological claim is that particular one on which was killed Jesus Christ whom the apostolic community proclaimed to be the same as the risen Lord. It bars cheap grace, and it bars romanticizing suffering.

A theology of this particular cross does not have as its subject matter suffering in general, or self-sacrificial love in general, or the vaunted power of powerlessness in general, or redemptive narrative in general. The cross is not in the first instance a symbol of the intersection of the heavenly and the earthly or of the horizontal and vertical dimensions of religious experiences. It certainly is not the opening for rationalizing yet another speculative theology — one which romanticizes and makes peace with powerlessness and suffering, which sanctions guilt and self-destruction, which makes palatable injustice and defeat.[10] On the con-

---

10. On the role of sloth in misconstruing suffering, see Monica Furlong, *Christian Uncertainties* (Cambridge, Mass.: Cowley, 1982), pp. 44-46: "A distorted Christianity has sometimes made a virtue out of being in pain, as it has made a virtue out of martyring oneself for a cause. I believe we should reject this masochistic device, and try instead to be happy and live as fully as we can, accepting suffering if it comes

trary, the particular cross of the proclaimed Jesus Christ redefines and corrects and provides the criteria for the church's right thinking and right practice; it is not some procrastinated heaven but here and now in the midst of the mundane suffering, injustice, sacrificial love, and ambiguity with which all humans are acquainted.[11] This particular cross, on which was hanged the mediator Jesus Christ, is the way of victory over sin, death, and the devil — then, now, and in the future. Hence the faith we confess: "Christ died, Christ is risen, Christ shall come again."

The implications of this continuity of the crucified and risen one are extensive. Here I mention three of the most important: what this means for the material of the resurrection, what this means for the relation between dying to sin and being a new creation in Christ, and what this means for the relation between the Old and New Testaments. These deal with three ways our salvation depends on that continuity.

The continuity of the crucified and risen one is essential to the salvific meaning of the resurrection.[12]

---

our way (as it does anyway) but becoming intensely suspicious of our motives if we are constantly unhappy. Chronic unhappiness and sloth are inextricably intertwined. The slothful settle into a condition in which they feel that nothing is asked of them except to suffer; and, though they may hate the suffering, they feel it absolves them from action, from trying to bring about change. Religion becomes the 'opiate' of which Marx complained, lulling them with soothing words about the creative value of suffering when they should be taking responsibility for initiating change. We are surprisingly bad at being happy, at selecting the paths in life which would bring us joy and fulfillment rather than the ones which bring us to pain and destruction. But, having observed this bias in ourselves, we can note that when we turn our suffering into a virtue we are steering too close to the sin of sloth. Collectively, sloth opens the way to tyranny and persecution. Individually, it turns people into tiresome miseries who have forgotten the joy of living. As always, it is worth getting wise to our own perversity."

11. That point is indelibly made by Dürer's woodcuts on *ecce homo,* in the background of which is the suffering servant described in the prophet Isaiah.

12. On the identity of the crucified one, the risen one, and the coming-again one, see Braaten, in *Christian Dogmatics,* 1:523ff. Moltmann puts it this way: "The fundamental event in the Easter appearances then manifestly lies in the revelation of the identity and continuity of Jesus in the total contradiction of the cross and resurrection, of god-forsakenness and the nearness of God. That is why the whole of the

The continuity of grace confronts, interrupts, and transforms other continuities and definitions of continuity. The continuity of grace is one of death and resurrection, a continuity of God's steadfast love and covenantal remembrance at work through radical discontinuities. There is a sense in which one must say that the gospel has more to do with discontinuity than continuity. After all, it is said that "Whoever is in Christ is a new creature. Behold the old has passed away." And "Who are my mother and my brothers?" and "Unless you forsake . . . you are not fit for the kingdom" and "I bring a sword" and "My peace I give to you, not as the world gives peace."

Obviously this kind of discontinuity belongs to the very heart of the gospel. That means, however, that the discontinuity is contained within the continuity of grace. The discontinuity is not absolute. There is a recognized identity of the crucified and risen one. A seed must fall into the ground and die — but the resultant plant is from the seed. There is body to those who share the resurrection — a spiritual body, whatever that might be, but a body nonetheless. Christ's resurrection is not, as some have called it, another creation out of nothing. Christ's resurrection is saving for us bodily, rational creatures because Christ gestated in the womb of Mary, bore the sins of the world in his body, took that body to the grave, and appeared to witnesses in his incomparably unique resurrection body. It is not nothing that is raised. The dead is raised.

The risen Lord was crucified to death: the one in whom the apostles put their trust was crucified under Pontius Pilate, dead, buried, de-

---

New Testament can assert that the disciples at Easter did not see a new heavenly Being of some kind, but Jesus himself. The Lord who is believed and proclaimed at Easter stands in continuity with the earthly Jesus who had come and been crucified — a continuity which must repeatedly be sought and formulated anew and can never be surrendered" (Jürgen Moltmann, *Theology of Hope* [New York: Harper and Row, 1967], p. 199). The way Moltmann speaks here of the resurrection ill comports, it seems to me, with another way he sometimes, mistakenly in my opinion, speaks of the resurrection as a *creatio ex nihilo,* which would minimize the humanity of Christ also crucified, dead, buried, and raised again, as also the material of the resurrection. To paraphrase Gregory of Nazianzus, what has been healed is that which has been assumed.

scended into hell, and it was only on the third day, in accordance with the Scriptures, that he was raised from the dead. Christ stopped living. Had there been a cardiac monitor, as there are with our sophisticatedly barbarous executions, the pattern on the screen would suddenly have become only the machine's own flat line. Christ's eyelids needed closing by someone else. There were no vital signs when he was taken down from the cross and put away in Joseph of Arimathea's grave. Rigor mortis set in. There is a break, an enormous silence, in Bach's B minor Mass between the *"et sepultus est"* and the *"et resurrexit."*

That Christ surely died we know from the accounts repeated and written down by the community re-created by the same, and now risen, Lord Jesus Christ. The radical discontinuity — of betrayal, of condemnation, of excruciating death, of the experience of utter forsakenness — is contained within the continuity of God's steadfast love through him who came that we might have life and have life more abundantly. Life is ultimately more abundant than death. The No is contained in the Yes. That is, life and affirmation mean taking up one's cross to follow Christ, mean cosuffering with him that we may be coglorified with him. We are baptized into a death like his that we may also have a share in his life. Dying to sin is part of living to God.

> What shall we say then: shall we continue in sin that grace may abound? No way! God forbid. For how can we who are dead to sin, continue to live in it? Don't you realize that all of us who were baptized into Jesus Christ, were baptized into his death? Therefore by baptism were buried with him into death, so that just as Christ was raised up from the dead by the glory of the Father, we too might walk in newness of life. For if we have been united with him in the likeness of his death, we will also be united with him in a resurrection like his. (Rom. 6:1-5, mostly RSV)

That leads to the question about what the continuity of the crucified and the risen one means for the relation between death to sin and being a new creation in Christ.

For one of the most thoughtful treatments of this question, we can profit from looking at Bultmann's reflections again.[13] Bultmann at times takes a neglected point and so overemphasizes it that its original veracity gets watered down. Such is the case with his view of the radically new which is ushered in with the proclamation of the gospel which includes the announcement that these are the end times, the end of history. Whatever else may be said by those who invoke his name, Bultmann does not make the new which is ushered in a matter of the uninterrupted extension of natural possibilities in humans to be open to the future. For Bultmann grace, especially in the form of proclamation, breaks into the present and shatters all false securities, all patent and subtle reliance on living according to the law, the letter and the flesh; grace breaks in and frees the person from the old self and for living the new life of the end of history.

That side of Bultmann needs to be reheard, because it is so clearly a major part of the gospel, and because his program of demythologization, while finally too extremely carried out, was so that the gospel — and not false scandals — might be heard by what Bultmann took to be modern men and women. The messages of the New Testament free a person, here and now, to live in the end times by effecting an existential identification with those who were confronted also by the inbreaking of eternity there and then. The story of history recounted in mythological terms there and then becomes real to me; I am struck that it is for me and is my story too, in my demythologized freedom for the future. Should anyone doubt the evangelical intent of Bultmann, reading, and hearing from the written form, his Marburg sermons will correct that doubt.

There are not a few things on which one must differ from Bultmann. The charges of fideism and occasionalism, usually brought by critics who are Roman Catholic, are not easy to discount. However that may be, my concern here is with the implications of the continuity of the crucified one with the risen one — beyond the difficult matter of

13. For Jüngel's appropriately appreciative note concerning the intent of Bultmann's program, see *The Doctrine of the Trinity* (Grand Rapids: Eerdmans, 1976), pp. 21-22.

whether Bultmann has, finally, a view of history in which one could know there was a crucified one, to say nothing of a view of history which does not reduce the resurrection to an occurrence of the faith of the disciples.

It seems to me that Bultmann never anticipated the extension of his thought to the position which assimilates others' narratives into my personal narrative. It seems to me that Bultmann takes as obvious a thereness and a theyness and a thenness to others' narratives, and that this overagainstness is integral to the encountering qualities of the gospel. There is a world of difference between the following two statements: (a) "The cross and the Easter event are my history, too" and (b) "It is because the cross and the Easter event speak to my condition that they have any reality and value — that is, cross and resurrection are noteworthy because they are familiar parts of my own personal narrative." Bultmann's usual teaching is the former, but he is subject to those who later can distort his thought into providing the rationale for the latter.

Where, however, Bultmann's expressions are indeed too hyperbolically unguarded, then the consequences must be rejected lest we lose the discontinuity, as well as the correct continuity, between my experience here and now and that of the disciples then and there. My personal narrative is, of course, the material with which I receive and which is transformed in the reception of the gospel; but my personal narrative is not canonical narrative. The canonical narrative of God's steadfast love at work in the cross and resurrection is the yardstick, the plumb line, for measuring our personal narratives to see whether they be gratifying ways of pointing to my own self with narcissist religious exercises, or whether they be even more gratifying ways of remembering and telling the *magnalia Christi* in our midst. The text from which Christ is rightly preached is the canonical narrative; the text from which we preach not Christ but ourselves is my glorious personal narrative.

Now to what the continuity of the crucified and the risen one means for the relations between Old and New Testaments.

In order to address that correctly, one needs to acknowledge one's place in the lineage of betrayal. Bach has it right in the chorales of the Saint Matthew Passion where the congregation repeatedly confesses,

"Who did this to you? It is I." Or take that shatteringly simple line of the recitative when Peter hears the cock crow again: "And he wept bitterly." Any blaming of others for the betrayal, any self-vindicating explanations, and any substituting comfortably morbid sentimentality for costly repentance are swept away. Such repentance is the way of those who embrace and interpret the Old Testament from their participation in the New Testament. The minute we — who belong to the priesthood of all believers sharing Peter's confession and betrayal and restoration — confess "Jesus Christ," we have made the most radical claim for the continuity of God's steadfast love with the people of the Old and the New Testaments. There is just no such thing as making that confession and avoiding the stumbling block that comes with it. "The stone which the builders have rejected has become the head of the corner" (Ps. 118:22; Matt. 21:42).

This continuity of costly grace is what we sing about in the hymn: "Christ is made the sure foundation. Christ is made the cornerstone." The costliness of the continuity of grace is what comes out in the first question and answer of the *Heidelberg Catechism:*

Q. What is your only comfort in life and in death? A. My only comfort in life and in death is that I belong, body and soul and in life and in death, not to myself but to my faithful Savior Jesus Christ, who at the cost of his own blood has fully paid for all my sins and has completely freed me from the dominion of the devil; that he protects me so well that without the will of my Father in heaven not a hair can fall from my head; indeed, that everything must fit his purpose for my salvation. Therefore, by his Holy Spirit, he also assures me of eternal life, and makes me wholeheartedly willing and ready from now on to live for him.

When one refers, as I have just done, to "the people of the Old and New Testaments," the singularity of this people is asserted. It is asserted against those who disclaim the term "New Testament" as a prejudicial misnomer. And it is asserted against those who practically if not officially wish to have the New Testament without the Old. Saying and meaning

"Jesus Christ" is confessing that this one Jesus of Nazareth, the crucified and risen one, is the Messiah prophesied and awaited by the church in the Old Testament. The relation between Israel and church is not the same as the relation between the Old Testament and the New; the relation of Israel and church is the subject of both Testaments. Israel and the church are not the same, though neither can be itself without the other.

Anti-Semitism and anti-Gentilism are both sins far more serious than cruel, ingenious intolerance; for in their opposite ways both are penultimate acts of distancing oneself from the Messiah. There is enough in the sacred Scriptures of Israel to see that the Messiah looked for has something to do with the peace and right ordering of all nations. A nationalism like that of other nations would be for Israel to want to return to their plea in 1 Samuel 8 that they want a king like all the nations around them. It would be to miss the characteristics of the shepherd king whom God graciously supplies. And there is enough in the books of the Old and New Testaments taken together to insist that the sought Messiah, "the coming one," is the promised Jewish Messiah. Christ is not Jesus' surname! He is the one whom faithful Israel, in the persons of Simeon and Anna, welcome into the temple, whose coming as a light to all nations frees one for a fulfilled and peaceful departure. Simeon is looking at the baby Jesus when he says, "Lord, now lettest thou thy servant depart in peace, according to thy word; for mine eyes have seen thy salvation, which thou hast prepared in the presence of all peoples, a light for revelation to the Gentiles, and for glory to thy people Israel" (Luke 2:29-32). Israel and the church are two forms of God's people, and both live expecting the Messiah. Israel looks for the coming of the Messiah, the church for the second coming of the Messiah.

The Reformed confessions are particularly insistent on this point, and in doing so usually follow Calvin's treatment of the differences between and similarities of the two Testaments. What finally holds the two Testaments together is that Christ is the subject pointed to in both. The substance of the old and the new covenant is the same, and there is one Mediator between God and humanity whether in the old or the new covenant. In fact, there is one Mediator between God and creation: Jesus Christ.

That does not mean that it is really Jesus Christ who is partly hidden and partly revealed behind every bush, text, and hymn in both Testaments. What we get, say, in 1 and 2 Samuel is not the story of Jesus instead of the stories of Saul and David and Nathan and Jesse and Bathsheba and Uriah and Absalom and those who got killed trying to catch the tipping ark of the covenant. It is rather that the fullness of those idiosyncratic experiences and the incompleteness of them point forward to, contain the promise of, the one Mediator between God and man whom the church with confessional retrospection knows to be the crucified and risen Lord.

But Christ is more than the common reference point for both sets of writings, the main criterion for pointing to what is canonical. Christ is that, of course, but only because Christ is the Word of God on which other words depend in order to be revelatory. This is what the first two "evangelical truths" confessed at Barmen are all about.

> . . . Jesus Christ, as he is attested for us in Holy Scripture, is the one Word of God which we have to hear and which we have to trust and obey in life and in death.
>
> We reject the false doctrine, as though the Church could and would have to acknowledge as a source of its proclamation, apart from and besides this one Word of God, still other events and powers, figures and truths, as God's revelation. . . .
>
> As Jesus Christ is God's assurance of the forgiveness of all our sins, so in the same way and with the same seriousness he is also God's mighty claim upon our whole life. Through him befalls us a joyful deliverance from the godless fetters of this world for a free, grateful service to his creatures.
>
> We reject the false doctrine, as though there were areas of life in which we would not belong to Jesus Christ, but to other lords — areas in which we would not need justification and sanctification through him.[14]

14. Barmen Declaration, in *The Book of Confessions,* Presbyterian Church, U.S.A., 8.11, 12; 8.14, 15.

Whatever else Romans 8–11 means, it is clear that — from a Christian point of view — God maintains his covenantal fidelity with Israel. There is no zigzag: God worked with Israel until the Messiah came plus a generation or two, and then God — cross yourselves, for the rest of the sentence taken alone is blasphemous — switched covenant partners to favor the Gentiles and rejected the Jews. Paul at least makes it clear that Israel remains God's chosen people, that the Gentiles get incorporated into the special people of God but are free from the ceremonial laws in doing so and cannot be restricted to becoming a sect of Israel. One reason for God's fulfilling his promise through the acts done by the apostles by the power of the Holy Spirit is to be a sign to call Israel to acknowledge her Messiah and a sign that the Gentile believers are children of Abraham and Sarah by faith.

The Flesh of the Word

In order correctly to identify which theology of which cross is at the heart of sane doctrine concerning God's holiness, we now address two forms of the same question: whether the Word made flesh is the same eternal Word by whom all things are made, and whether the flesh assumed is that of Mary, Theotokos.[15]

Few have given as much prominence to the theology of the cross as Luther, and few have been as stubborn about its particularity. In case anyone should miss the point, Luther was ready to thump the table with a stein of good Saxon ale: "I neither know nor have any other God than that flesh which was gestated in the womb of the Virgin Mary."

Christology does not come up somewhere along the line after we

15. Parts of this section have been drawn from two lectures: one given on the occasion of the San Mateo (Calif.) Presbytery's deciding whether or not to admit as a member of the presbytery a person who no longer held to the truth of the incarnation, and one given on the occasion of the Karoli Reformed University, Budapest, celebrating 1,000 years of the founding of Hungary, with conferring degrees as part of that celebration.

have established God's identity and will; Christology has not so much to do with how God, whom we know from some other source in advance, is present in the person and work of Christ. Christology has to do with identifying the God whose name is Holy. Christology in a theology of the cross is presupposed from the outset, either explicitly or implicitly, no matter the order in which other matters are taken up. In Luther's case, he was fully aware that he was working with the Scriptures as interpreted by the Council of Chalcedon: Mary is God-bearer, which means that in knowing and having only the God of this flesh is saving doctrine, the opposite of what otherwise would be blasphemy.

The truth of the incarnation is an essential part of the confessional heritage — tradition — by which men and women are guided in their vocation to reconfess the faith of the one, holy, catholic, apostolic church today.[16] As part of the catholic church, the Reformed tradition teaches that the eternal Word of God, by whom all things were made, became flesh, dwelt among us full of grace and truth, taught and healed and proclaimed the kingdom, was obedient unto the death of the cross and was raised in victory over sin and death and the adversary, and is presently active by the Spirit as the head of the church, our only mediator and advocate, and the servant Lord over the world. Our greatest and only comfort in life and death is that we belong to him, are bound to him to enjoy his freedom, by the power of the Spirit who equips us in the joyful struggle to live lives of ultimate trust in him.

That the truth of the incarnation is expressed in confessional, doxological language does two things simultaneously. It ties the experience of wholeness (salvation, therapy, forgiveness, liberation, empowerment to walk in newness of life) to the person and work of Jesus Christ as God living humanly. And it evokes levels of experienced meaning of

---

16. On the relation between culture and Christianity illumined by pursuing the implications of seeing Christ as the embodied cosmic Logos, see Werner Jaeger's summary lectures entitled *Early Christianity and Greek Paideia* (Cambridge: Belknap Press of Harvard University Press, 1961), pp. 65ff., on Origen, and pp. 68-102 on the Cappadocians. Note G. L. Prestige's concise treatment of holiness and transcendence: *God in Patristic Thought* (London: SPCK, 1952), pp. 21-28.

that wholeness which, while tied to a particular formulation, goes to levels not conveyed by just a literal sense of the language.[17]

The confession that Jesus Christ is the eternal Word, by whom all things were made, living humanly is one of several complementary faith-claims about the person and work of Jesus Christ. "Jesus, Christ" and "Jesus, Lord," "Son of Man," "Son of God," "the Coming One," "the Lamb of God who takes away the sins of the world," "Mediator," "High Priest," "Immanuel," and so on are all responses evoked from the community which is constituted by God's liberating and empowering Word. That Jesus is the eternal Word, by whom all things were made, the light which enlightens all persons, become flesh — this confession is neither to displace the other ways of speaking of Christ nor to be relinquished. It belongs to the richness of the biblical witness to Jesus as the Christ, and serves that richness. Its denial, or even diminution, constitutes a serious reductionism of the range and depth of ways we respond to God's being for us and the whole world as Jesus of Nazareth. Its reconfession, which inevitably includes newly appropriated language and media for successive cultural contexts, serves to proclaim the inclu-

17. In this latter claim I am using what is sometimes referred to as the "symbolic" character of theological language. I am chary of the overuse of the term "symbol" just because all too often "symbol" is taken popularly to mean you get something "instead of the real thing." Confessional language is "symbolic" only in the sense that the reality it points to and participates in is so compellingly experienced that there occurs a gracious polarity which shatters and transforms previously expected categories and possibilities. Symbolic language in this sense only serves to locate — but not to exhaust — the mystery of God's being uniquely for us in Christ. If one chooses to use "symbol" in this connection, then at least one should specify Tillich's sense of the term, as that which participates in the reality to which it points and which has a kairotic power which we finally do not choose and control. Even more helpful is the careful use Ricoeur makes of the term: "I define 'symbol' as any structure of signification in which a direct, primary, literal meaning designates, in addition, another meaning which is indirect, secondary, and figurative and which can be apprehended only through the first" (*The Conflict of Interpretations: Essays in Hermeneutics* [Evanston, Ill.: Northwestern University Press, 1974], pp. 12-13). There is no bypassing the primary meaning: the symbolic meaning is given power by the function of the first meaning to provide the analogue which brings about the analogy.

sive purposes of precisely that God who encounters us as person in Jesus Christ.

Within every branch of the catholic church, the fundamentals of the faith require active remembrance, redefinition, reinterpretation — all of which actions belong to the faithful delivery of the faith from generation to generation. There are periods, seasons, when what one thought could be taken for granted suddenly are evidently subject to several forms of obscurity. They may be simply ignored, especially where there is no solid liturgy for kinesthetic memory; they may be caricatured into teachings which would not be even slightly recognizable to their original authors; and they may be wittingly opposed in their misshapen form. This does not mean that we are left with a cynical view which would see any form of doctrinal development as an instance of doctrinal devolution. On the contrary, doctrinal development is one of the many realms of which it must be said that in the darknesses light shines. The confession is not so much that the light shines after the darkness *(post tenebras lux),* but that in the darknesses the light shines *(in tenebris lux).*

What I am about to say about the doctrine of the incarnation according to the Reformed tradition does not apply to that tradition alone — else it would not be part of the catholic tradition! There may indeed be some special emphases on which Reformed theologians have insisted christologically — and we will turn to them in due course. First, though, it is necessary to register the ways in which the Reformed heritage is *not* distinctive either in what it teaches about the person of Jesus Christ or in the doxological and confessional forms in which it does so.

There is considerable richness to the way the incarnation and (the inseparable corollary) the Trinity are taught in Reformed confessions. Here I need only refer to the places where those teachings are most explicit and recommend that the range and power of those confessions on these points be recalled. The Nicene article is always in the back of the mind of subsequent confessions, though their formulations are not restricted to the language of substance in which it was stated.[18] The Bar-

---

18. Constitution, in *The Book of Confessions,* 1.2; Scots Confession, 3.06; 3.07; *Heidelberg Catechism,* 4.016–4.019; Second Helvetic Confession, 5.015–5.019;

men Declaration and the Confession of 1967 do not undertake to restate a summary of the faith, but presuppose and align themselves with the creeds and confessions which explicitly confess, among other things and central to them, the incarnation and the Trinity. The preface to the Confession of 1967 makes clear that its aim is not to treat all traditional topics of theology. "For example, the Trinity and the Person of Christ are not redefined but are recognized and reaffirmed as forming the basis and determining structure of the Christian faith." The confession does not mince words, however, in specifying the implications of those doctrines for confessing God's reconciling work and presence. "In Jesus Christ, God was reconciling the world to himself. Jesus Christ is God with man. He is the eternal Son of the Father, who became man and lived among us to fulfill the work of the Holy Spirit to continue and complete his mission. This work of God, the Father, Son, and Holy Spirit, is the foundation of all confessional statements about God, man, and the world. Therefore the church calls men to be reconciled to God and to one another" (9.07).[19]

5.062–5.079; Westminster Confession, 6.011–6.013; 6.043–6.050; *Westminster Larger Catechism,* 7.146–7.152.

19. In *The Book of Confessions,* 9.07. Although it did not become a part of the Constitution of the Presbyterian Church, U.S.A., the proposed (1976) Declaration of Faith has been fairly widely used for teaching purposes and is interesting for its effort to confess the faith in narrative form. It obviously also confesses the triune God and the incarnation (1:4; 4:3; 6:2), and does so in a particularly dynamic way. The same prominence is given to the incarnation and Trinity in recent confessions of Reformed churches around the world. Examples of this are to be found in the collection edited by L. Vischer (entitled *Reformed Witness Today* [Bern, 1982]) for the World Alliance of Reformed Churches, two-thirds of whose member churches are from the third world: the antiapartheid 1979 Declaration of the Broederkring of the Dutch Reformed Church, and Declaration of Faith for the Church in South Africa, of the Presbyterian Church of South Africa; the Common Comprehension of Faith of the Council of Churches in Indonesia, 1967; the 1981 Confession of the Church of Toraja; the Confession of Faith of the Kyodan (United Church of Christ in Japan), 1954; the New Confession of the Presbyterian Church in the Republic of Korea, 1972; the Confession of Faith of the Presbyterian Church in Taiwan, 1979; the Confession of the Presbyterian-Reformed Church in Cuba, 1977 ("God's incarnation in Jesus of Nazareth

We need now to mention something which has long been *alleged* to be "a distinctive" of Reformed theology, alleged, that is, by those who — with a whole range of political, territorial, economic reasons — had great interest in driving a wedge between Reformed theology and catholic theology. That falsely alleged distinctive was the so-called Calvinistic extra.

The best way to dig again with profit in what would otherwise be only a well-tramped-down archaeological site, is with the question which identified the real issue at stake. This was a soteriological one, and within that, it was a question of how indeed humans could be subjected to the grace of God — how could the ordinary means of grace be applicable to us. For the Reformed that meant the question of how the preaching of the Word could be in any way God's very own presence in our midst. The question is not, "How can we get grace so we can preach better?" That question is frightèningly close to Simon Magus's about the Spirit in Acts. The question is, "How ever can we forgiven sinners in all honesty say, 'Hear the Word of the Lord,' and accurately mean the Scriptures and our preaching the gospel out of them?"

The Second Helvetic Confession (chap. 1) teaches that the preaching of the Word is the Word of God. Such a teaching is founded on the reality of the eternal Word's having become flesh, the personal union of true God and true man. Preaching becomes a form of the Word of God only because the eternal Word became flesh, to whom, Jesus Christ, we are united by the bond of the Holy Spirit and faith.[20] I want therefore to

---

and the liberating vocation this fact implies for the Church constitutes the spiritual foundation for the historical commitment to which the church feels it is called"); the Constitution of the United Church of Zambia, 1965; the Basis of Union of the Church of South India, 1941; the Plan for Union of the Joint Commission on Church Union in New Zealand, 1971; the Basis of Union of the Uniting Church in Australia, 1979; and the Basis of Union of the United Reformed Church in the United Kingdom, 1981. This last one is of particular interest for the exercise of doctrinal *episkopē* by presbyteries when it says, "The faith to be confessed has thus to be expressed in terms that can be voiced by those who come from any of the three [uniting] traditions. The central evangelical confession was not difficult to reach, because each of the three church bodies stood in the orthodox trinitarian tradition" (Vischer, p. 465).

20. Cf. Calvin, *Institutes of the Christian Religion* 3.1 and 3.2.

call attention to the correct reading of one much-debated sentence, and call attention to what is at stake in the truth or falsehood of the sentence.

The sentence is: "In the incarnation the eternal Word was united to the flesh in such a way that he, the eternal Word, continued to be also beyond *(etiam extra)* this flesh."

The issue is: whether the eternal Word became flesh in such a way that he ceased his provident care for the whole of creation.

Reformed theologians have held the sentence to be true. They have insisted that the same Word who became flesh for redemption is the very same Word by whom all things were made and by whom all things are providentially sustained, accompanied, and governed. Calvinists have taught that the eternal Word is united to the flesh but is not restricted to the flesh: is united to *"sed etiam extra"* the flesh. They have insisted on this connection between providence and redemption so much that, in seventeenth-century polemics, some Lutherans coined the phrase "the Calvinistic extra" *(illud extra calvinisticum).*

Elsewhere I have done some work showing that this label is a misnomer, that the teaching is patristic and catholic, that its rejection was a novelty of Lutheran (not Luther's) polemics, and that the *extra patristicum* is still a necessary teaching. Here, however, I want mainly to call attention not to the <u>extra</u> *patristicum aut calvinisticum* but to the <u>etiam</u> *patristicum aut calvinisticum.* The words "united . . . but also" *(sed etiam)* make it perfectly clear that the main point is the *personal unity* of the divine and the human in Christ. The "also beyond" is an explication of that unity: it is not a kind of unity which reduces the one to the other, or a kind of unity in which one absorbs the other. The four famous Chalcedonian adverbs *(inconfuse, immutabiliter, indivise, inseparabiliter; asunchutōs, atreptōs, adiairetōs, achōristōs)*[21] specify the uniqueness of this unity. They identify what at the very least we are saying the incarnate Word, Jesus Christ, is.

As J. C. O'Neill has pointed out, the meaning of the prologue to John's Gospel is that the Word by whom all things were made was made flesh. That is a far stronger claim than the common translation that the

---

21. Denzinger, *Enchiridion Symbolorum,* 31st ed., pp. 70-71.

Word became flesh. The Word is not reduced to flesh; and the flesh of the incarnate (enfleshed) Word does not become a third thing, neither Word nor the flesh of creatures. To use the language of the ecumenical councils, the one person Jesus Christ is the union of the divine and human in such a way that: the person and work of Christ can never be separated; being human surely includes the flesh; and the life, death, resurrection, and awaited coming again of the enfleshed Word are ultimately the only sufficient revelation of who God is and what kind of person this encountering God is. That is, union of Word and flesh is not the same as identity of Word and flesh. That means the so-called economic Trinity is not exactly, coterminously, exhaustively the so-called immanent God. The God who reveals Godself in the incarnation is prior to us and to all creation in every way of time-space-velocity-energy. The revealed God is the one in whom we live and move and have our being — not the other way around, as if our existence defined God's being. It is not we in whom God lives and moves and has God's being, though the boundless God surely and freely indwells us as an action of sovereign grace.

Classic Reformed Christology on this point is a restatement of the Chalcedonian Christology in terms which are appropriate to subsequent economic, social, intellectual, and psychological contexts. That Christology is not one which describes an already living Jesus becoming indwelt by the divine Spirit or even indwelt by the divine Word. The Chalcedonian Christology describes the incarnation of the eternal Word who — in Athanasius's terms a century before Chalcedon — "contains all things and is contained by none."[22] The eternal Word takes up — the assumption of *carnis*[23] — our condition and in his whole obe-

---

22. Athanasius, *De incarnatione* 5.

23. Cf. Gregory Nazianzus, *Ep. ad Cledonium, M.J.,* in *Enchiridion Patristicum,* ed. Rouet de Journal (Barcelona: Herder, 1959), p. 381. Though strangely unfamiliar to some modern theologians, the christological model of "assumption" is one of the most influential ones, being the one used for the structuring of Barth's doctrine of reconciliation, vol. IV of the *Church Dogmatics,* and for Saint Thomas's questions 3 through 6 of the third part of the *Summa theologiae.* Cf. D. Willis, "The Conditions of Experiential Dogmatics," *Princeton Theological Seminary Bulletin,* New Series 2, no. 3 (1979): 232-50.

dience, death, and resurrection heals and restores the effaced-by-sin image of God in which all human beings are created. The classical Reformed Christology is not a response to a general question, "How can the finite contain the infinite?" The classical Reformed and Chalcedonian Christology is a response to the fact that the finite is taken up into the life, the *energeia,* of the infinite Triune.

We need to recover the _etiam_ *calvinisticum* for the way it functions to correct a false understanding of transcendence. It also functions to nourish a correct understanding of the efficaciousness — the vital reality, the *res vivens* — of the ordinary means of grace; but of that, more later. The _etiam_ *calvinisticum* helps get the discussion of transcendence back on the right track. It obviates two prevalent alternatives: one which misunderstands and exaggerates divine immanence, and one which misunderstands and exaggerates divine transcendence.

The _etiam_ *calvinisticum* is a necessary teaching today over against those who, first, separate divine transcendence from divine immanence; who, second, seem unaware that immanence and transcendence necessarily imply each other; and who, third, emphasize immanence at the expense of transcendence (who even speak of "the transcendent God" *and* "the immanent God"!) or the other way round. The exaggeration of immanence misunderstood results in pantheism, the teaching that God is the sum total of everything: there really is no distinction between Creator and creature. The exaggeration of transcendence misunderstood results in atheism that does not even bother to argue against God's existence: by definition God is inconceivable, is totally absent even if he is, and is utterly beyond the changeableness, corruption, and multiplicity of observable phenomena. Neither pantheism (of the Eutychean or the Plotinian variety) nor what I can only call "absentheism" (of the Arian or the radically materialistic variety) has the prophetic leverage necessary for living as God's people in this, God's, world.

CHAPTER TWO

Communio Sanctorum

As the previous section makes clear, when we turn now to Christ joined to his belongings we are not in any way abandoning the centrality of the doctrine of the Trinity for probing the meaning of God's holiness. If anything, focusing on Christ and his belongings makes the trinitarian material all the more evidently compelling. In this I have only to add a gloss, and a small correction, to Barth's own gloss on what the doctrine of the Trinity means for the procedure of theological reflection on holiness.

On the subject of the holiness of God, as on so many topics, Barth's organization of material and bold reinterpretation of it are as compelling as they are dialectically thorough. I am persuaded by his argument that God's attributes are technically God's perfections, and I am mindful that the structure of his argument in *Church Dogmatics* II/1 is a masterful way of analyzing different aspects of an indivisible subject. It has usually been my experience that when a person wishes to make a corrective point to one of Barth's emphases, it will turn out that Barth himself has somewhere anticipated that move and suggested better ways to make the point himself! That is not to say that there are no differences of proportion and formulation, and false starts, to be noted. However, I am convinced by Barth's seeing God's holiness as primarily a perfection of God's love (para. 30) rather than primarily a perfection of God's freedom (para. 31). I think, however, that Barth pulls back too soon, and unnecessarily, from spelling out the implications which the singular holiness, according to his own treatment, has for manifold holiness. I think, for example, of the matter of *creaturely consecration, the holiness of creaturely diversity. To think through and suggest a robustly positive — not a cautionary negative — relation between the Holy One and the holy many* is a daunting task which is not often the main concern of Reformed theologians, but one in which today one must sin boldly if the field is not to be left to the hosts of romantically inclined pantheists.

One of the primary strengths of Barth's teaching is his insistence that the grace of God and the holiness of God are related as the love of God and the freedom of God. Accordingly, our idea of God's holiness will grow as our idea of God's mercy grows.

> We have already recognized this in presupposing the great reciprocal qualification and expansion of the two leading ideas of the love and freedom of God. In doing this we did not postulate a cleavage and dualism in God, but were obliged and wished to respect the unity of God in the clearness and fulness of His revelation and being. We must adopt the same procedure at every point in the details as well. We will therefore make the kind of distinction which does not imply a second factor alongside a first, but simply wishes to recognize the one according to the clearness and fulness with which it is a unity in God. We are not, then, making any crucial change of theme when we go on to speak of God's holiness. We are merely continuing to speak of God's grace.[1]

Barth goes on to spell out what this means by emphasizing the transcendence of God, his freedom according to which he is and always remains Lord, maintaining his will over against every other will. "God's loving is a divine being and action distinct from every other loving in the fact that it is holy. As holy, it is characterized by the fact that God, as he

1. Karl Barth, *Church Dogmatics* II/1 (Edinburgh: T. & T. Clark, 1957), pp. 358-59.

seeks and creates fellowship, is always the Lord. He therefore distinguishes and maintains His own will as against every other will. He condemns, excludes and annihilates all contradiction and resistance to it. He gives it validity and actuality in this fellowship as His own and therefore as good. In this distinctiveness alone is the love of God truly his own divine love."[2]

This strong passage invites comment on Barth's use of *will* and *transcendence* in defining God's holiness.

Here Barth is drawing heavily on the language about the will of God versus human will in bondage. There is a harsh edge and a clashing of wills in Barth's teaching here which could lead either to reinforcing good news or its perversion into bad news. In Barth's hands it is good news. Barth is moving here (in *Church Dogmatics* II/1) toward (in II/2) his brilliant treatment of election as part of the doctrine of God. God's will which is maintained over against every other will is that all men and women be elected and rejected — in that unequal order — in Christ. That is the importance of using *Gnadenauswahl,* and of always thinking grace when speaking of election even if it is not always said. This move, of course, is pleasing neither to (a) those who need to deny the ultimacy of mercy (even if it includes the manifest experience also of rejection) nor to (b) those who need to deny God's mercifully overruling human wills gone devilishly awry (even if it is God himself who most suffers evil's consequences). Barth errs, if this indeed be recognizable error, on the side of the sovereignty of mercy.

I am less persuaded by Barth's treatment of *transcendence* in this passage than I am of his use of will. My objection is that he does not follow his own method far enough and bring to bear on *the relation between holiness and transcendence* the mutuality and expansion he sees in *the relation between love and freedom* and in the *relation between grace and holiness.* In other words, I think Barth — at least in this important passage — still reinforces too much the alignment of God's holiness with transcendence as God's freedom over his creation, and does so at the expense of the nearly as important alignment of *God's holiness with*

2. Barth, p. 359.

God's transcending presence also within his creation. There is an important nuance here which is expressed, in English, in the difference between speaking of God as "the Wholly Other" (which the early Barth favored as a remedy against domesticating God) and as "the Holy Other" (which I favor and which is surely the logic of the later Barth's corrective in *The Humanity of God*). It is because of God's gracious choice not to be totally other *(totaliter aliter)* that we know God to be the One Holy Other *(alius unus sanctus)* who confronts us as purifying love.

Though I would add that caveat to Barth's teaching, his procedure is fundamentally correct insofar as he insists on the point that Christology and the doctrine of God are simply sides of the same church doctrine. Those who play theocentrism off against Christocentrism depend on a tacit agreement that, when you come right down to it, Nestorius was right after all: the divine and the human are present but not fully united in the one person Jesus Christ. This disjunctive mentality is a symptom of amnesia about the point of the *theologia crucis:* the only way to be theocentric, and not idolocentric, is to be christocentric. True theocentrism, that which focuses on the living Triune, is christocentric.[3]

That, at least, is what Luther and Calvin mean when they say that when it comes to the assurance of salvation, we are to look neither to ourselves nor to our works, but we are to gaze only on Christ. Apart from Christ there is no assurance of anything. Well, there is something: labyrinthine aimlessness, the prison labor *(ergastulum)* of fantasy.

---

3. That does not mean that the entirety of the theological enterprise is Christology, which, I think, is what several of the less nuanced of the self-consciously "theocentrists" seem to be objecting to. One sometimes gets the impression that what are being set against each other are not so much theocentrism and Christocentrism as theocentrism and Jesumonism. Catholic theology, however and obviously, is not a Unitarianism of the Son, any more than it is a Unitarianism of the Father or of the Holy Spirit. That is, Christology is not reducible, without skipping the Chalcedonian adverbs, to Jesusology — as if we could in fact have the so-called historical Jesus apart from the proclaimed Christ, who through the Word and Spirit continues to encounter us as the once crucified, now risen, and coming-again Lord.

Surely the assurance of salvation depends neither on the results of self-examination, nor on the perpetuity of our own personal faith, nor on an impressive string of displayable good works.

In the same breath one must add that true faith does indeed bear fruit, fruits of costly discipleship, fruits good because they are acceptable in God's sight for Christ's sake. Such is the way of costly grace, lest one run again into confusing (a) assurance of salvation for Christ's sake alone with (b) the opulent lassitude of cheap grace. It is as members of the body of Christ that we realize and act out our freely given and freely assured salvation.

Christ and His Belongings

The central question here is whether by the bond of the Holy Spirit believers are actually united to Christ and thereby united to one another into a holy communion.

To keep the various dimensions of the *communio sanctorum* in perspective, it is helpful to keep together as a unit the questions (53-58) of the *Heidelberg Catechism* dealing with the third article of the creed and the questions (59-61) dealing with justification by faith alone.

Q. 53. What do you believe concerning "the Holy Spirit"? A. First, that, with the Father and the Son, he is equally eternal God; second, that God's Spirit is also given to me, preparing me through a true faith to share in Christ and all his benefits, that he comforts me and will abide with me forever.

Q. 54. What do you believe concerning "the Holy Catholic Church"? A. I believe that, from the beginning to the end of the world, and from among the whole human race, the Son of God, by his Spirit and his Word, gathers, protects, and preserves for himself, in the unity of the true faith, a congregation chosen for eternal life. Moreover, I believe that I am forever and will remain a living member of it.

Q. 55. What do you understand by the "communion of the saints"? [Note that the German shares with the Latin the double meaning of holy persons and holy gifts.] A. First, that believers one and all, as partakers of the Lord Christ, and all his treasures and gifts, shall share in one fellowship. Second, that each one ought to know that he is obliged to use his gifts freely and with joy for the benefit and welfare of other members.

Q. 56. What do you believe concerning "the forgiveness of sins"? A. That, for the sake of Christ's reconciling work, God will no more remember my sins or the sinfulness with which I have to struggle all my life long; but that he graciously imparts to me the righteousness of Christ so that I may never come into condemnation.

Q. 57. What comfort does "the resurrection of the body" give you? A. That after this life my soul shall be immediately taken up to Christ, its Head, and that this flesh of mine, raised by the power of Christ, shall be reunited with my soul, and be conformed to the glorious body of Christ.

Q. 58. What comfort does the article concerning "the life everlasting" give you? A. That, since I now feel in my heart the beginning of eternal joy, I shall possess, after this life, perfect blessedness, which no eye has seen, nor ear heard, nor the heart of man conceived, and thereby praise God forever.

Q. 59. But how does it help you now, that you believe all this? A. That I am righteous in Christ before God, and an heir of eternal life.

Q. 60. How are you righteous before God? A. Only by true faith in Jesus Christ. In spite of the fact that my conscience accuses me that I have grievously sinned against all the commandments of God, and have not kept any one of them, and that I am still ever prone to all that is evil, nevertheless, God, without any merit of my own, out of pure grace, grants me the benefits of the perfect expiation of Christ, imputing to me his righteousness and holiness as if I had never committed a single sin or had ever been sinful, having fulfilled myself all the obedience which Christ has carried out for me, if only I accept such favor with a trusting heart.

Q. 61. Why do you say that you are righteous by faith alone? A. Not because I please God by virtue of the worthiness of my faith, but because the satisfaction, righteousness, and holiness of Christ alone are my righteousness before God, and because I can accept it and make it mine in no other way than by faith alone.

This freely given forgiveness is at work in deeds of love. There is, according to Calvin, a kind of double justification: not only are we sinners justified by grace alone through faith, but the works of the freely justified are also freely accepted by God despite their obvious incompleteness and imperfection — just as parents take delight in, and plaster the walls with, the partial and idiosyncratic crafts offered by their beloved children.

In explicating his definition of faith, Calvin repeats the claim that it is only in gazing on Christ that we have assurance of our acceptance by God. This is in book 3, chapter 2 of the *Institutes*. In doing so, however, Calvin gives an easily missed but highly significant twist to what it means "only to gaze on Christ." He distinguishes between "looking to Christ only" and "looking to Christ alone." We must look to Christ only, but we cannot look to Christ alone. There is, for us, no Christ alone — only Christ united to his body.[4]

Institutes 3.2.24 is crucial in Calvin's clarification of what he means — and does not mean — by teaching that one of the characteristics of

---

4. Much of the remainder of this paragraph appears in "The *Unio Mystica* and the Assurance of Faith according to Calvin," in *Calvin: Erbe und Auftrag* (Festschrift for W. Neuser), ed. W. van't Spijker (Kampen: Kok Pharos, 1991).

true faith is that it is "firm and certain." The passage is also crucial to Calvin's identifying what he means — and does not mean — by that which is the foundation of the assurance of faith, namely, union with Christ. One of the arresting things about this passage is the way Calvin goes beyond the position which is assumed to be his. He agrees with those who insist that when it comes to the assurance of faith we must focus on Christ, not ourselves. However, he puts his finger on the consequences of not taking that correct focus far enough, so that believers may not be buffeted alternately by fear and hope. The right kind of self-knowledge is part of the material of the assurance of faith. Or, to put it the other way round, the correlation between the knowledge of God and knowledge of self (in which practically all our knowledge consists [*Institutes* 1.1.1]) means that a corrected knowledge of God involves a corrected assurance of faith.

This section is typical of the process by which the *Institutes* grew into the final edition of 1559-60. Calvin added this section in the 1543 and 1545 editions to elucidate the definition of faith he gave in his 1539 and 1541 editions: ". . . a firm and certain knowledge of God's benevolence towards us, founded on the truth of the freely given promise in Christ, both revealed to our minds and sealed on our hearts by the Holy Spirit."[5] That does not mean that faith is not frequently tossed about and mixed with doubt. It only means that no matter how almost extinguished it may seem, God keeps faith alive in believers, who by definition are simply those who look for their assurance to Christ. That is clear: the assurance of faith comes from focusing on Christ and not on ourselves apart from him. More must be said, however, in order not to draw from this consequences which would undercut that assurance.

Calvin's doctrine of the union with Christ is one of the most consistently influential features of his theology and ethics, if not indeed the single most important teaching which animates the whole of his

---

5. *Institutes* 3.2.7; in *Johannis Calvini Opera Selecta,* ed. P. Barth and W. Niesel, 5 vols. (Munich: Chr. Kaiser, 1926-36), 4:16 (hereafter *OS*); *Institution de la Religion Chrestienne,* ed. J.-D. Benoit, 5 vols. (Paris: J. Vrin, 1957-), 3:23 (hereafter CIB); *Institutes of the Christian Religion,* ed. J. T. McNeill, trans. F. L. Battles, 2 vols. (Philadelphia: Westminster, 1960), p. 551 (hereafter CIM).

thought and his personal life.[6] As is often the case with a fundamental assumption which influences a thinker's work at every point, there is a richness of language used in describing it that can be confusing. This is particularly true when it comes to what is meant by the union with Christ, and especially when Calvin calls it the "mystical union," given the perplexing — and often simply contradictory — interpretations given to the term "mystical" in the history of Christian thought.[7] Evaluating Calvin's use of the doctrine of the union with Christ is a matter of tracing the way it functions differently in different contexts; but Calvin is quite clear about what the union with Christ is.

To understand what Calvin means by it, we must note the difference between two levels of that union. The second or consequent level of union presupposes the prior or first level of union.

There is the incarnation, the hypostatic union of the eternal Word with the humanity which believers share with every other person. The

---

6. Of the literature on this topic, see especially: W. Kolfhaus, *Christusgemeinshaft bei Johannes Calvin* (Neukirchen: Buchhandlung des Erziehungvereins, 1939); W. Niesel, *The Theology of Calvin* (Philadelphia: Westminster, 1956), esp. chap. 9; W. Krusche, *Das Wirken des Heiligen Geistes nach Calvin* (Göttingen: Vandenhoeck & Ruprecht, 1957), esp. pp. 265-72; F. Wendel, *Calvin: Origins and Development of His Religious Thought* (New York: Harper and Row, 1963), pp. 234-42; C. Partee, "Calvin's Central Dogma Again," in *Calvin Studies,* Papers of the 1986 Davidson Colloquium, ed. J. Leith (Richmond: Union Theological Seminary, 1986), pp. 39-46; B. Armstrong, "Duplex cognitio Dei, Or? The Problem and Relation of Structure, Form, and Purpose in Calvin's Theology," in *Probing the Reformed Tradition,* ed. E. McKee and B. Armstrong (Louisville: Westminster/John Knox, 1989), pp. 135-53.

7. See W. R. Stiktberg's thesis done in 1951 at Union Theological Seminary, New York, "The Mystical Element in the Theology of John Calvin," and W. Kolfhaus's section on "Christusgemeinschaft, nicht Christusmystik," in Kolfhaus, p. 125. It is a fair summary to say that as Calvin treats it, "this mystical union is always ethically polar (an expression of the relation between Lord and servants), corporate (taking the form of co-membership in the church), and eschatological (an accomplished fact but never perfect in this life)" (in D. Willis, "A Reformed Doctrine of the Eucharist and Ministry and Its Implications for Roman Catholic Dialogues," *Journal of Ecumenical Studies* [spring 1981]: 295-305, here p. 298).

"communication of properties" applies to this level, the hypostatic union, which is primarily the subject of *Institutes* 2, chapters 13 and 14.

There is, secondly, the particular union of Christ with believers which comes about by the Holy Spirit who is the bond by which we are united to Christ (*Institutes* 3.1.1), the eternal Word made flesh. This is the reality which Calvin, in a subsequent section (3.11.10), calls "that conjunction of the Head and members, the indwelling of Christ in our hearts, the mystical union."[8] The "marvelous exchange"[9] by which what is Christ's becomes ours applies to this second level of union. It is this particular union of Christ with the members of his body that Calvin is

---

8. "That conjunction of the Head and members, the indwelling of Christ in our hearts, the mystical union [Fr., sacred union by which we rejoice in him] is given the highest importance by us, so that Christ, having been made ours, makes us sharers in the gifts with which he has been endowed. We do not therefore consider Christ from afar or outside us, that his righteousness might be imputed to us; but because we are clothed with him and engrafted into his body — in short, because he chose to make us one with him — we glory in the fellowship we have in his righteousness" (*OS,* 4:191; CIB, 3:214; CIM, p. 737). In this section Calvin is contrasting his view with Osiander's. The latter's seems to be that Christ's substance is communicated to us (Calvin also teaches that) — but in such a way that the distinction between the reality of Christ and the reality of the believer is obliterated. When Calvin uses the word "substance" of what is communicated to us of Christ, he means the reality, the *res,* of Christ. Calvin, however, does not want to relinquish the term "substance" — and especially not in controversies about the Lord's Supper — lest we be misunderstood as saying that something less than that the reality of Christ himself is communicated to us. The benefits of Christ are communicated to us only and insofar as Christ himself is communicated to us. See D. Willis, "Calvin's Use of Substantia," in *Calvinus Ecclesiae Genevensis Custos,* ed. W. Neuser (Frankfurt am Main: Lang, 1984), pp. 289-301.

9. "Mirifica commutatio" in (*Institutes* 4.17.2) one of the sections on the nature and benefits of the Lord's Supper. The section begins, "Godly souls can gather great assurance and delight from this sacrament. In it they have a witness of our growth into one body with Christ so that whatever is his may be called ours. Consequently, we may dare assure ourselves that eternal life — of which he is the heir — is ours, that the kingdom of heaven into which he has already entered can be no more shut off from us than from him, and that we cannot be condemned for our sins from whose guilt he has absolved us since he willed to take them upon himself as if they were his own" (cf. CIM, pp. 1631-32).

speaking of when he says (here in 3.2.23), "The reason we hope for salvation is not because he appears to us from afar off but because having engrafted us into his body [Fr., 'united us to his body'] he makes us participants not only in his benefits but also himself." This particular union — I repeat — presupposes the prior union. It is the way believers have applied to them the salvation wrought by "the whole course of obedience" (2.16.5) of Jesus Christ, the eternal Word united to humanity.

Calvin notes the view of some — he calls them demi-papists — who draw false consequences from this union. Their argument, as Calvin presents it, is a strong and appealing one. They reject one view of how doubt and faith are related, namely, that of those Scholastics who understand faith just to be doubtful opinion.[10] For that error, however, they substitute another by teaching that assurance of faith is always mixed with doubt. They indeed acknowledge that when we look on Christ we have all the material for good hope. However, they argue that since we are still unworthy of the benefits offered us in Christ, looking on our own unworthiness causes us to waver and hesitate. "In short, they so place the conscience between hope and fear that now it moves in one direction and now another. They see hope and fear related in such a way that when the one is up, it completely extinguishes the other, and when it is the other's turn it does the same. . . . Their contention is, if you look upon Christ there is sure salvation, if you turn back to yourself, there is sure damnation. As if indeed we ought to consider Christ remaining apart from us instead of living within us!"

> The reason we hope for salvation from him is not because he appears to us from afar off, but because, having engrafted us into his body [1545: "united us to his body"], he makes us participants not only in his benefits but also in himself. Using their own argument — namely, when we look upon ourselves we look upon our damnation — we come to a very different conclusion. Since

---

10. The 1560 edition (CIB, 3:42) thus identifies what the 1559 calls (*OS*, 4:34) "the crude doubt" (simply, *crassa dubitatio*) taught by "the schools" which these "half-papists" reject.

Christ has been communicated to us with all his benefits, so that what is his has been made ours and we are made members of him and made one with him [1545: "made of one substance with him"], his justice covers our sins, his salvation wipes out our damnation, his worthiness interposes itself so that our unworthiness does not come before the face of God. This is for sure: we ought neither to separate Christ from ourselves nor ourselves from him, but with both hands hold fast to that fellowship by which he has bound us to himself [1545: "to that union by which he has united us to himself"]. Thus the apostle teaches us, "Now your body is dead because of sin; but the Spirit of Christ which dwells in you is life because of righteousness [Rom. 8:10]." . . . He teaches that that condemnation which we of ourselves deserve has been swallowed up by the salvation that is in Christ. And to confirm this, he uses the same reason I have advanced: that Christ is not outside us, but dwells within us. Not only by an inseparable bond of fellowship does he hold fast to us, but by a certain marvelous communion he daily grows more and more with us into one body, until he finally makes himself one with us [1545: "daily he more and more unites himself to us in one, same substance"].

Calvin then adds, in the 1559 edition, the following reminder: "However, I do not deny what I said above, namely that from time to time some interruptions of faith occur, insofar as its weakness is buffeted here and there among violent blasts. So, in the thick darkness of temptation its light is snuffed out. Nevertheless, whatever comes about, it does not leave off earnestly seeking God."[11]

11. *OS*, 4:35; CIB, 3:42-43; cf. CIM, pp. 570-71. The reference to faith being snuffed out in the density of testings is not to be minimized as part of Calvin's own experience. The assurance which comes from knowing oneself to be united to Christ as a member of his body has existential import for one who knew anxiety as well as Calvin did. See also that fine section on what it means that we belong not to ourselves but to God (3.7.1), and see Zanchius and Ursinus's most memorable question 1 of the *Heidelberg Catechism*: "What is your only comfort in life and in death? A. That I be-

We noted above the difference between looking at "Christ only" and looking at "Christ alone." "Christ alone" is an abstraction, an item for speculative theologies of glory, something we simply have no access to apart from Christ's remembering and reconfessing and rehoping community and its writings. "Christ to whom we look only" is the Christ accommodated and continually accommodating to our condition,[12] the Christ united to his body by the bond of the Spirit, the Christ who is sovereign head of the church and Lord of all the world, the Christ whose service in every area of life is perfect freedom. The Christ only on whom faith focuses is, to use the distinction Calvin used,[13] the *"totus Christus,"* the knowing and serving of whom is the content of comembership in his body.[14]

The Material Work of the Holy Spirit

The question here is whether or not there is a plurality to holiness. That is, does holiness so strictly belong to God alone that it cannot be a shared reality, or does purifying love include newly becoming what God declares creatures to be? Does not the reality of the *communio sanctorum* imply and express a pneumatological, covenantal, and declarative understanding of being? To get at this question, in this section we will consider the interconnection between the continual work of the

---

long — body and soul, in life and in death — not to myself but to my faithful Savior, Jesus Christ, who...." W. Bouwsma's intriguing portrait of Calvin (*John Calvin* [New York: Oxford University Press, 1988]) does a service in considering the various possible roots for the anxiety of the sixteenth-century person (pp. 32-48), even though one might wish for more attention given also to Calvin's assurance of faith and its foundation.

12. See F. L. Battles, "God Was Accommodating Himself to Human Capacity," in *Readings in Calvin's Theology,* ed. D. K. McKim (Grand Rapids: Baker, 1984), pp. 24-42.

13. *Institutes* 4.17.30 and passim.

14. See P. Lehmann, *Ethics in a Christian Context* (New York: Harper and Row, 1963), pp. 63-73 and 102-23, on the Reformers' doctrine of the communion of saints and the trinitarian foundation of ethics.

Holy Spirit in redemption and the continuing work of the Holy Spirit in creation. We do so in that order, redemption and creation, because it is as we experience the course of redemption that we are able rightly to identify and confess the one Holy Spirit also ceaselessly at work through creation — and to distinguish the one Holy Spirit from the many spirits.

We have seen that, according to Calvin, the Holy Spirit is the bond by which people are united to Christ. By this Calvin means primarily that believers are united to Christ. They are believers not prior to that unity, but by that unity are made new creatures and are given the gift of faith — mainly through the Word, the sacraments, and church discipline — by which we grasp the benefits freely promised and lavishly delivered. If asked how the Holy Spirit effects that union and makes the Word and sacrament and discipline efficacious, we can say (true as far as it goes) more than that it just happens: for Calvin, to say something is real is to say it is spiritual, because it is the Holy Spirit who unites things otherwise separated in time and space.

This union of things separated in time and space has its ground in the prior and inner being of God. It is a fact of the accommodation of the Holy One. These transforming and uniting actions are heftily real, have gracious space and density and momentum, are the matter of creation and redemption because of the prior reality: the eternal Love of God coming to expression by accommodation in the act of the triune God to create and redeem.

The Word and the Spirit are never separate, either in eternity or in time. The eternal Word become flesh is present and active by the power of the Holy Spirit, and the Holy Spirit is present and active by the power of the eternal Word by whom all things are made. Sanctification is thereby not just a matter of forgiveness of sins hypothetically divorceable from the restoration-plus of the image of God into which humans are created. And it is a false, counterfeit spirituality of creation which flirts with nature romanticism in general apart from knowing that propaedeutic experiences are penultimate and are experiences of grace only because they are anticipatory tastes of the ultimate who is Jesus Christ, the saving enfleshment of the eternal Word by whom all things were made and in whom all things shall be recapitulated at the end.

Both the redeeming and the creating work of the Holy Spirit are simultaneously material and spiritual. That is, we must be vigilant against assigning the work of *Spiritus Creator* to something loosely thought of as the material realm, and the work of *Spiritus Redemptor* to some realm that is by definition nonmaterial. All the human senses and physical elements, for example, are involved in the Spirit's moving people to faith and in their growth as freely and perfectly forgiven sinners. And the Spirit's universally provident care includes the benevolent intent for the whole of creation, spiritual and physical, whether of believers or not, whether of humans or not. The faith of believers in Christ is embedded in the matrix of the physical world; matter no less than spirit is redeemed, and the way of redemption is through physical elements taken up and used by the Word and Spirit no less than through spiritual elements. In fact, it is extremely difficult, and perhaps thoroughly misleading, to perpetuate a distinction between spirit and matter unless one means to distinguish simply between the visible and the invisible dimensions of creation — a distinction which, as we shall see, depends on what portion of the spectrum of God's being the Holy Spirit makes visible to us without ever reducing the whole spectrum to what we perceive.

That is why it is too Docetic, attenuated, and prissy to balk at the *epiklēsis* in the liturgy of the Lord's Supper, which beseeches the Holy Spirit to use the elements and not just the people assembled. Why ask for the Holy Spirit to come upon sinful humans but not upon other physical creatures? Obviously, the celebrant's words are not spoken to the elements of bread and wine; but the Holy Spirit brings the elements and people together, unites what was separated, blesses, consecrates, sets aside from an ordinary to a special use the creatures in the believing community's act of worship. To be sniffy about the *epiklēsis* betrays the same dualistic and Manichean propensity — the "spiritualizing" proclivity — which prays that the hearts of men and women may be changed but is not robust enough to dare to pray for the economic, political, ecological dynamics which faith also presupposes. A reconciling faith of the reconciled community is one in which the Spirit unites the things which are otherwise separated, and the Spirit's use of humans and of the creatures of the elements is an effective sign of God's reconciling purposes for the whole of creation.

We are not here speaking of another work of the Spirit than the principal one of quickening and sustaining and guiding the faith of members of the body of Christ. The efficacy of the Word to bring about the gift of faith is the work of the Holy Spirit. It is not a question of first being given faith and thereby, then, being able to profit from the Word and the sacraments. Rather, that is the way faith comes about — through the Spirit's use of the materiality of the Word.

See, again, what the *Heidelberg Catechism* says of faith's whence:

Q. 65. Since, then, faith alone makes us share in Christ and all his benefits, where does such faith originate? A. The Holy Spirit creates it in our hearts by the preaching of the holy gospel, and confirms it by the use of the holy Sacraments.

Q. 66. What are the Sacraments? A. They are visible, holy signs and seals instituted by God in order that by their use he may the more fully disclose and seal to us the promise of the gospel, namely, that because of the one sacrifice of Christ accomplished on the cross he graciously grants us the forgiveness of sins and eternal life.

We will return to this part of the *Heidelberg Catechism*. Here we need only note the astounding fact which so easily passes us by when outlandish claims of holiness become domesticated religious jabber. "Holy" is applied, in this passage, adjectivally to plural signs, the sacraments; the gospel preached by freely forgiven human beings is called "holy." Holiness is not the opposite of creatureliness but is the right use of creatureliness. Humans are rightly used, as humans and not as bodiless rational creatures (which is what angels are), in the preaching of the gospel.[15] Bread and wine and the water do not get in the way of a fo-

15. On the significance of the holiness of ministry, see the treatment of conse-

cused faith in Jesus Christ. They are means, mediating instruments, by which God's good favor and efficacious forgiveness are conveyed and appropriated historically. That is why Luther says if you want to find Christ, go to the *Gemeinde,* to the gathering of those who ride on Christ's shoulders.[16] There is plural holiness when applied to the holy people, the forgiven sinners growing in grace, and the plurality of holiness modifies the ordinary means of grace.

Holiness in the plural is, moreover, used in another sense, to which we now turn: the things which are to be shared as part of Christians' common ministry.[17]

Life Together

The *Heidelberg Catechism*'s section on this, quoted above, bears repeating here. "Q. 55. What do you understand by 'the communion of saints'? A. First, that believers one and all, as partakers of the Lord Christ, and all his treasures and gifts, shall share in one fellowship. Second, that each one ought to know that he is obliged to use his gifts freely and with joy for the benefit and welfare of other members."

Believers share in, are partakers of, Christ and his benefits, which benefits are never divorced from his person. Out of that one fellowship believers, freely and with joy (see Calvin's *"sponte"* of Christian free-

---

cration and baptism into Christ's ministry in Thomas Torrance, *Royal Priesthood* (Edinburgh: Oliver and Boyd, 1955), pp. 73-87.

16. There is an iconographic reversal here. Christ carries Saint Christopher and carries us, and our faith is our bold reliance on that transportation over troubled waters.

17. On *communio sanctorum* as "communion of saints" and "communion in holy things," see Jan Milič Lochman, *The Faith We Confess* (Philadelphia: Fortress, 1984), chap. 16. On "holy" and "holiness," see Xavier Léon-Dufour, ed., *Dictionary of Biblical Theology,* 2nd ed. (New York: Seabury Press, 1973), pp. 236-39; Klaus Hemmerle's article "Holy," in *Encyclopedia of Theology,* ed. Karl Rahner (New York: Seabury Press, 1975), pp. 639-41; and Gordon Lathrop's companion volumes, *Holy People: A Liturgical Ecclesiology* (Minneapolis: Fortress, 1999) and *Holy Things: A Liturgical Theology* (Minneapolis: Fortress, 1993).

dom), have a joyful obligation — a thanksgiving duty — to use their gifts, which are really Christ's, for the benefit and welfare of other members. It is through the fellowship that Christ's treasures and benefits are passed on to others and received from others in a joyful, free, continual exchange. That is what constitutes life together in Christ, to whom we are united by the influence, power, joy, nurturing, and perseverance of the Holy Spirit.

This passage does not spell out what "gifts" believers are to share with one another. Since these gifts derive from Christ's and his treasures (not the treasury of merits of the saints; note also here Calvin's imagery for prayer as that by which we dig up the treasures of Christ [*Institutes* 3.21.1]) and benefits, at least the gifts of the Spirit are intended. Even more clearly, though, given the section on the communion of saints with which this passage deals, the gifts are what Paul refers to in his description of the body of Christ: each member is gifted according to the measure of Christ's gifting for the sake of the whole body. There is an ordering, a discipline, to this life together, as each member performs the function for which he or she is gifted and does not denigrate, despise, or make a class structure out of the sane diversity of gifts.

There is no superiority or inferiority of persons based on what they perform, since each gift is by Christ's own measuring. And we recall from another context that rank and preference among the disciples is defined by Christ's own servant Lordship, the foot washing by the one to whom they are united by the power of the Spirit. Hence, love one another as Christ has loved you and given himself; and welcome one another as Christ has welcomed you. He who though he was rich yet for our sakes became poor that we through his poverty may become rich. This "wonderful exchange" by which we share in Christ and his benefits means that the life together of believers itself is an effective sign of the last days ushered in by Christ, is an effective sign of the life which God wills for all in these end times.

And what has this to do with sharing physical belongings? Everything. This fact of fellowship and consequential caring through sharing Christ and his benefits is the defining beginning, the *archē,* of Christian thought and action about the distribution of the goods of this world, including what the civil law calls "property." We are still treating the topic of the *communio sanctorum*. We have not abruptly turned to the topic of the commonwealth of nations, though we have turned to how the fellowship of believers illumines how Christians are to think and act for the commonweal.

There are two immediate implications of this principle. One deals with what belonging to Christ has to do with belongings. The other deals with what delight in the goods of this world has to do with their proper use.

The first implication is that believers understand that they and what they have been given belong not to themselves or to others but to Christ: believers are Christ's stewards of the goods of this world. The second is that the sharing of spiritual gifts includes physical, material, nourishing, healing, delighting, freeing things — and sharing the accountability which goes with this social realism. Both make sense only when we put as frontlet between our eyes justification by grace alone through faith. That is, the whole communal dynamic is the loving interaction of freely forgiven sinners who are justified by grace alone through faith, and whose good works are justified by God's acceptance of them as the thanksgivings of members of the body of Christ.

There are immediate social and economic consequences of confessing one's belonging to Christ. "My belongings" is an odd phrase for believers to use, as is "my personal property." The terms are permissible when engaging in the civil (first) use of the law. Strictly speaking, however, we understand ourselves to be stewards, engagers in husbandry, responsible keepers in the household of God, of self, of others, of other creatures, of our neighborhood — the earth and its galactic proximities. The whole belongs to God, the God we know definitively through the cross of the risen Lord to whom we are united by the bond of the Holy Spirit.

This belonging to God alone is exactly the same as freedom to be for another and freedom to be oneself in community: that includes the freedom to accept others being for us and the freedom of others to be for themselves. There follows a subaltern, entrusted sense of belonging which has to be taken with joyful seriousness: the relations between parents and children. Actually, children do not belong to parents — nor parents to children. Yet they are "our children" and "our parents" in the sense that those in question are entrusted to the others, and this entrustment is another word for the responsibility and stewardship of a loving community. That love is an in-season and out-of-season thing, in those times when the loving is reciprocal and when it is not. The same applies to the estate of marriage. Strictly speaking, spouses do not belong to another; yet it is true that they freely give themselves to each other and endearingly speak of my husband and my wife.

In both cases — and in other contexts of stewardship where subaltern, entrusted belonging is acknowledged and embraced — there is no room for the idea of a person being some other creature's "property." That is what is diabolical about slavery in any form — even, or especially, in its paternalistic and maternalistic guise: it is an acted-out form of coveting that which belongs to God alone. It is insisting that an earthly master's or mistress's voice be heard, trusted, and obeyed in the place of the one Word of God which everyone alike is freed to hear, trust, and obey in life and in death.

Life together is sharing Christ and his benefits: this is the organizing reality, the principal fact *(archē)*. We have been dealing with the first implication of this, and have said something about the senses in which belonging to God alone sheds light on other belongings. Now we turn to the other implication, in order to say something about the "goods of this world" which are shared and for which members of the body of Christ are stewards.[18]

Calvin takes sharing the goods of this world so seriously that he includes it in what was circulated as a separate booklet on the Christian life. In the final edition of the *Institutes,* this chapter is placed in the book which spells out the ramifications of our sharing Christ's person and benefits by being united to him and to each other by the power of the

---

18. Compelling instances of this particularity are the prayers (e.g., that of the grandmother of Brother Banks cited on pp. 36-37) transmitted and commented on in Harold A. Carter, *The Prayer Tradition of Black People* (Valley Forge, Pa.: Judson, 1976).

Spirit. This sharing Christ entails the *duplex gratia* — justification and sanctification — and Calvin puts his full-fledged treatment of sanctification (or regeneration, or repentance) first in order to show how full of good works is this freely given justifying faith (which means he has all along put justification first). He then gives his readers his full-fledged treatment of justification in order to show that the Christian life is, from beginning to end, a matter of Christian freedom (which is the content of sanctification all along). In the construction of his argument in book 3 of the *Institutes,* Calvin is thus following an order of teaching which is at once an instrument of rhetoric and persuasion as well as a dialectically mutual way of defining both parts of the twofold grace which is ours by virtue of our being united to Christ and other members of his body by the power of the Holy Spirit.

For our present purposes there are at least three things to be noted about Calvin's treatment of the right use of the goods of this world.

First, the goods of this world are to be shared, not to be rejected or wasted. This is a dicey business, for the use of worldly goods can easily become a rationalization for growing inordinately fond of them if you accumulate them and for covetousness if you cannot gain them — or wish not to gain them and thereby be relieved of the freedom to use them responsibly. Erich Fromm's *Escape from Freedom* is as pertinent a warning now as ever; ditto T. S. Eliot's treatment of the third, not just the first or second, temptation in *Murder in the Cathedral.* Full-bodied testing — temptation — comes with the possibility of the use or abuse of worldly power, be that power economic, political, sexual, psychological, spiritual, or — as usually happens — differing combinations of all these plus a few other kinds. The temptations lie at least as severe — because all the more apparently humble — on the side of refusing to exercise the power of whatever kind a person may be given. The two extremes are always there: the burgher's assurance of election by piling up profits, or the manipulative habits of the well-heeled who practice being (in John Ciardi's terms) the "weak by trade who bait the best of their betters with a mock helplessness." In this perilous tension, Calvin's experiment in Geneva was an elaborate effort to care for the material side of the reform of society no less than of the church. The goods of this world are good because they are gifts of God who is good (no Manichean denigration of creation at this point); but they are good in their proper use for the commonweal for which they were intended, namely, for the alleviation of the condition of the poor, needy, persecuted, suffering. In this sense there is indeed a worldly asceticism — to use Weber's language — in the positive sense of mundane stewardship rather than fleshly aggrandizement.

Second, right use includes taking right delight in the goods of this world. Use and delight are not set over against each other. They are mutually definable. Joyless stewardship is an oxymoron. The joy of stewardship is not the avoidance mechanism of determined euphoria, of pretending "peace, peace" where there is no peace and "happiness, happiness" where there is no happiness. The joy of stewardship is what Mother Teresa is about when she notes that serving the miserably dying in Calcutta includes a certain kind of joyful self-forgetfulness which focuses on the detailed, particular care for the person literally on one's hands, literally to uphold this person on God's behalf. We will return to this paradoxical relation between delight and service in the chapter on the holiness of beauty.

Third, the Decalogue functions as a guide for the complex matter of discerning the difference between the use and the abuse of the goods of this world, of discerning the difference between sane delight in the goods of this world in their correct use and insane bondage to rampant materialism rationalized religiously. How the Decalogue functions this way without leading to legalism or to persnickety earnestness is a matter of perennial debate over the prominence given to this, the third use of the law, in Reformed theology. That is, besides the civil use of the law and the use of the law to drive us men and women to repentance, there is a continuing use of the law to guide men and women in the exercise of Christian freedom. I leave a fuller discussion of this to the sixth chapter when we consider the ordinary means of holiness.

CHAPTER THREE

The Eternal Love of the Holy Other

By starting with the theology of the cross, this treatment of holiness began candidly with two prominent confessional presuppositions. They are that God makes Godself to be known by humans, and that the foundational reason for trusting the knowability of God is the eternal identity of the Holy Trinity. These mean that revelation is not just *about* God. Revelation is God's triunely *self-evidencing* by creating and redeeming, triune activities which are reliably congruent finite reflections of God's infinite being. The theology of the cross is not, in the first instance, an anthropology of the cross or a cosmology of the cross, though they also follow. The theology of the cross is theology because the Subject who is actively obedient there is the enfleshed eternal Word of God.

It will not do to have a definition of revelation which completely excludes communication of propositional truths — which exclusion, incidentally, is usually put propositionally. Nonetheless, revelation is primarily to be understood as I-Thou encounter. This implies that the encountering Subject is at least partially knowable. Now, if the encountering one discloses himself or herself (the pronouns are personal if one is to stick to the analogical language of I-Thou encounter) to be benevolent and trustworthy rather than their opposites, the partial knowability is sufficient for salvation.

Revelation is indeed not primarily the thought and articulated experience of something *about* God, though these are blessed consequences. Revelation is the self-evidencing *encounter* initiated and sustained by the infinite Subject, whose encounter elicits the response by the derivative subject being given existence through this encounter. The finite response includes the intellect and the tongue and propositionally expressed truths, though limited and fragmentary and partial, so that seeing through a mirror obscurely is still accurately locating that which, or the one who, is reflected. This is not unlike traces left by subatomic particles. The vestiges, the track left by neutrinos which are themselves invisible, are accurate indices of the dynamics of the thereby presupposed reality; the vestiges are not just vestiges of vestiges of vestiges ad infinitum. It is the triune God who makes Godself to be experienced triunely; what is also made known in revelation is not just human experience of human experience of human experience ad infinitum.

In this chapter we shall seek to say something accurate about the conjunction between who God is and the response to this encountering God; put otherwise, we shall seek to say something accurate about how the church comes to confess with the mind and lips that which it knows by heart: God's eternally being triune.

Being eternally love: that is who God is essentially, and that is what being holy means. The present chapter intends to examine the components of this claim.

The Procedure of Pure Love to Purifying Love

In this study I choose to treat eternal love, pure love who is God, first and then to treat timely love, purifying love of creation and redemption. I am fully aware that in the order of human knowing the procedure is different: the sequence of knowing goes from experienced manifestation to the reality manifested. However, I have made my choice in order to make it as clear as possible that *the being of God is the inclusive reality, and the derivative existence of the creature is the included reality. Utterly singular holiness proceeds. By this totally free procession, plural and derivative holiness is created, taken up, and sustained.*

My reason for this arrangement of the material is the same that Calvin gives for placing, in book 3 of the *Institutes,* the main section on sanctification before the main section on justification. Calvin chooses this arrangement to show that free justification by grace alone through faith does indeed result in the practice of holiness, although throughout — including in the dedicatory letter to Francis I — Calvin affirms the priority of justifying grace, growth in which constitutes sanctification. The previous generation of reformers made the case that sinners are freely justified for Christ's sake alone. Now, in Calvin's generation, the need was to make clear that the new life in Christ is not just a nominal, inefficaciously declarative change. Calvin preferred to speak of the "order of teaching" rather than any inherently logical structure of his thought, and in this respect also I am aware of the parallel between his treatment of justification-sanctification and my treatment of pure love–purifying love.

The case has been amply made that we know God from God's self-disclosure, God's presence and work *ad extra.* That is what the *theologia crucis* is all about in the order of knowing — that knowing which knows God to be prior to our knowing. Now the complementary case has to be made again: that in the order of being, *who God is* precedes *knowing who God is and who we are.* The point of beginning, as we have, with the cross of the risen Christ is that right knowledge of this particular God must inevitably start with God's self-disclosure, which is God's going forth *ad extra.* It is, however, of particular urgency today to make clear that the God we thus know by revelation is prior to our knowing, and that our knowing takes place within the encompassing, including knowledge which God has of us in Christ. Growth in holiness can be said, in this way, to be discovering more and more God's knowledge of us good creatures who are freely forgiven sinners.

In considering the doctrine of the Trinity, it has been a common practice to deal with God's unity, then with the three *hypostaseis* of that unity, and finally with the *perichoresis* as a tool to keep together the equally important affirmations of God's unity and relations both *in se* and *ad extra.* I am departing from that familiar arrangement and am beginning with a restatement of the doctrine of the *perichoresis*.[1] I do so to make it as clear as possible that God's unity *is* the triune *perichoresis* — God's eternally being relational, God's eternal presence to Godself, the utter simplicity of God's being eternally pure love. We can then turn to identifying some of the temporal, spatial, and energetic consequences — some of the salvific ramifications — of God's being eternally pure love.

The doctrine of the divine *perichoresis* functions salvifically in at least three complementary ways. Each way is a variation and extension of the central, binding function: that the believer enjoy the assurance of God's loving beneficence and, with creaturely diversity, reflect back the Triune's glory. The three complementary functions are: (1) to make more brilliant the realization that as eternal love, God's being is dynamic (the subject of this chapter); (2) to make more brilliant the realization that God's eternal presence is inclusive of God's temporal presence (the subject of chapter 4); and (3) to make more brilliant the realization that the utterly unique holiness of God elicits the idiosyncratically diverse holiness of creatures (the subject of chapters 5, on the holiness of beauty, and 6, on the hope of holiness).

Before we can deal with these salvific functions we need, however, to identify *perichoresis* as the dynamic of God's being triunely the Holy Other.

The Simplicity of Relational Being

God's holiness is the all-embracing, all-encompassing attribute of God — or, in the language of perfections, the holiness of God is the perfection of all God's perfections.[2] That is, there is nothing more perfect that

---

1. See Barth's historical excursuses on *perichoresis* in *Church Dogmatics* (hereafter *CD*) I/1 (Edinburgh: T&T Clark, 1936), pp. 425-26; on the doctrine of relations, pp. 419-21; and on persons, pp. 408-11. See Jüngel's discussion of the use Barth makes of the doctrines of "appropriation" (and *opera trinitatis ad extra sunt indivisa*) and *perichoresis,* in *The Doctrine of the Trinity: God's Being Is in Becoming* (Grand Rapids: Eerdmans, 1976), pp. 26-29.

2. On Trinity, being of God, and attributes of God, see Robert W. Jenson, in

comparison with would yield a definition of God's holiness. Holiness is the dynamic simplicity of God who is love.

The first word when it comes to perichoretic teaching is "adoration."

The initial and perennial response to God's dynamic being-unto-Godself is awe, wonder with the content not of shriveling revulsion but of incomparable — literally incomparable — transforming beauty. Adoration in this sense is synonymous with worship, with doxology of one's whole being in different patterns and differing degrees of fullness at differing seasons of one's life and in differing patterns of doubt, struggle, and ambiguity. Human doxology (we are not here speaking of angelic doxology, which also has — as the liturgy reminds us — its own place) includes the activity of reason more and more restored and more and more healed in the presence of the one being adored.

Adoration is not just an attitude tacked onto knowledge; adoration is the mode of knowing trinitarianly, corresponding to, apt for, congruent with the Subject about whom we are daily given the freedom to reflect and to speak and to practice obedience. We know that the words, thoughts, analogies used to point to one to whom we are freed to respond are straw. And we know, therefore, that adoring silence is by far the most reliable response to the disclosed mystery of God's being. But there is also the spoken silence which is evoked by this heart knowledge, the spoken silence, the articulate wonder, which expresses the reality of being affectively encountered by the disclosing one. The Sanctus is sung by seared lips. Accuracy about the vision counts in the activity set off by the vision.

Christian Dogmatics, ed. Carl Braaten and Robert W. Jenson, vol. 1 (Philadelphia: Fortress, 1984), pp. 135-91. On attempts to define God's substance and the efforts to distinguish between the substance of God and his invariable attributes, and how this effort was expressed in terms of God's transcendence and immanence, see Christopher Stead, *Divine Substance* (Oxford: Clarendon, 1977), p. 166. Note also the importance attached to holding these together in the structure of "The Moscow Statement Agreed by the Anglo-Orthodox Joint Doctrinal Commission," 1976 (London: SPCK, 1977), p. 82; and G. L. Prestige, *God in Patristic Thought* (London: SPCK, 1952), chap. 2.

The doctrine of the divine *perichoresis* serves this reflective and articulate dimension of adoration, because it is one of the most accurate ways of pointing to the essentially dynamic being who is eternally love. The Holy Trinity's being is pure act and pure simplicity, which is exactly the same as holiness. This simplicity is defined by its being uniquely actualized toward another through the love manifested in the particular cross of Jesus Christ. The being presupposed in this movement from a theology of the cross to a sane understanding of the holiness of the Triune is dynamic. I repeat: *perichoresis* refers to the eternal dynamic of this absolutely simple love who is the Holy Other One.

When we consider the attributes, or perfections, of the Triune, we are not pondering the attributes of deity in general. Nor are we equating the "attributes" of God with the "persons" of the Trinity. Nor are we attempting, by default or by intent, to apportion some of the attributes more to this person than to another person. Even to toy with this approach is already to give "person" a sense of a social entity in a way which teeters on the edge of the abyss of tritheism, which is no more excusable in its modern than in its ancient forms.[3] The attributes are not character traits of this God, nor are they additional features, alongside the three eternal ways of God's being one. The attributes of God are the "by-us considerable" uniquenesses, properties, *idiomata* of this God.

Several venerable Reformed orthodox theologians wrote much, well, and diversely about the perfection, or attribute, of God's holiness. They by no means offer us a single way of treating the topic. Even when the propositional language may be similar from one theologian to the

3. On *hypostasis, prosopōn, persona,* person and personality, see Barth, *CD* I/1, pp. 408-11. Barth quotes Calvin's words (from *Congrégation de la divinité de Christ,* Corpus Reformatorum, 47:473), which I here translate: "The ancient doctors made use of the word 'person' and said that in God there are three persons, not at all what when talking in our ordinary language we call three men, three persons — or, even as in the papacy they would dare paint three puppets [*marmousets*] and there you have it, the Trinity! But in this matter, the word 'persons' is used to express the properties which are in the being [*l'essence*] of God." Barth also notes J. Gerhard's warning (in *Loci* 1610 I.III, 62) that between human persons familiar to us and the divine Persons there is a *magnum imo infinitum discrimen* (Barth, *CD* I/1, p. 410).

next, the differing systematic locations of their treatments point to significantly variable emphases in their teachings. We can profit, in the present discussion, from examining and translating what some of the erstwhile Reformed orthodox theologians meant when they held to the teaching that *God is pure act and pure simplicity.*

Variations in the doctrine of divine holiness can be arranged according to: the constancy with which these theologians recognize holiness to be the perfection of all other perfections or attributes; and the constancy with which they spell out the implications of this teaching for the systematic ordering of their other teachings. We can discern three gradients or types of their treatments. There certainly are more types, but there are at least these three.[4]

First, there are those who consider the holiness of God under another locus, such as the absolute will of God. Here the will of God is given such controlling prominence that God's holiness is treated as the purity of God's affections or as a supreme virtue.

---

4. The perceived weaknesses of the bulk of orthodox Reformed theologians are described by their critics in terms which are often contradictory yet assumed to be synonymous. It is not unusual to encounter the judgment that these older Reformed orthodox theologians were too "speculative" and "static" rather than "experiential" and "dynamic," "abstract" rather than "concrete," "essentialist" rather than "existentialist," "dialectical" rather than "rhetorical," "philosophical" rather than "biblical," "theoretical" rather than "practical" — and so on. While the jargon used in these assessments is notoriously vague and question begging, there is usually at least some modicum of truth in even the most hyperbolic of generalizations. The lumpy labels stuck on the older Reformed orthodox are no exception. One must admit that would-be champions of Reformed orthodoxy serve their cause ill when they sometimes give the impression that a nostalgic reduplication of Reformed orthodoxy is an adequate substitute for the critical appreciation — the candid agreement and disagreement, the informed sifting and weighing — which these theologians deserve. Nonetheless, we would impoverish the doctrine of God were we to ignore many of the insights of these theologians who, in their own contexts and with their own language, were dealing with serious and perennial issues. These issues have not gone away just because we moderns or postmoderns (or so-called postfoundationalists whose foundational tenet is that the earlier theologians were fundamentally wrong) are not interested enough, or do not have the requisite disciplined creativity, to keep up with most of the Reformed orthodox.

This type has much to recommend it. When we define God's holiness as pure love, we shall be using parts of the legitimate insights of this type. Its drawback is that it too easily makes the affections, and ultimately the will, of God an external measure by which to define perfection. This is the case with Mastricht and Heidegger, to whose fuller view we shall presently turn. I think I am correct in saying that for Cocceius, veracity is the defining term for God's holiness: God is true to God's word. The word is covenantally efficacious for us because there is no falsehood or dissimulation in God.[5] Even here, though, the primary referent of the truth which God loves is the perfect love who is Godself.

Second, a variation of the first, there are those among the older Reformed orthodox whose approach is a combination of two teachings: (a) that God's holiness and righteousness are the same, and (b) that righteousness is to be understood in juridical — law-giving and law-fulfilling — terms.

The first part of this combination is correct if not tautological. The second part, however, allows (but does not necessitate) a particular understanding of law to be the controlling term for defining God's holiness. This is closely allied with a rather curious way of presupposing unrighteousness or iniquity, the absence of which in God defines holiness. If pushed too far, this would mean that the absence of imperfection is what we mean by holiness or perfection of love. This would be to define holiness as the privation of iniquity, rather than the other way around. Even here, though, a person like Riissen[6] or Turretin obviously holds that by law is meant the absolute will of God, so that it is God's holy will that makes law holy.

The third emphasis (or third feature, more dominant in some Reformed orthodox than others) sticks most consistently with defining

---

5. Heinrich Heppe, *Reformed Dogmatics* (Grand Rapids: Baker, 1978), p. 92 (hereafter *RD*), cites Cocceius, *Summa Theologiae* 3.10.52: "Holiness consists in God's necessarily loving truth and saying and doing nothing by which to deny or obscure truth."

6. Cited in Heppe, *RD*, p. 92: "It is righteousness and holiness by which without any *iniquitas* God is all that He is" (Leonard Riissen, *Compendium Theologiae Didactico-Elenchticae*, III, 38).

holiness and perfection strictly in terms of each other, so that the simplicity of God is the same as God's being unalloyed or unmixed with contrarieties. Bullinger has it right when he treats the bad not as a thing in itself but as a privation of the good.[7]

Of those quoted in Heppe, however, it is Mastricht who most concisely exemplifies this third feature of Reformed orthodoxy's treatment of divine holiness. The passage is worth citing at length.

> Holiness belongs to God (1) not as an accessory but as His actual essence; nor (2) as something received from another source but as the fountain of holiness in all things (Lev. 20:8; 21:15; Ezek. 20:12 ["I am the Lord who makes holy . . ."]; 1 Thes. 5:23 ["The peace of God sanctify you wholly . . ."]); nor (3) by fixed measure; but without measure in an infinite degree, which accordingly cannot be increased or diminished because this is its very essence, although it can and ought to be declared more and more (Mt. 6:9 ["Hallowed be Thy Name . . ."]); nor (4) fashioned after the holiness of the law, or anything, but as the idea and pattern and norm of all holiness (1 Pet. 1:15 ["Like him who called you is holy . . ."]; Eph. 4:24 ["The new man who after God has been created in . . . holiness . . ."]); and not so much (5) as a particular attribute of it, but as a universal affection, affecting all and any of its attributes; not, in a word, (6) some common *affection* of it, but by far the chief.[8]

7. Cf. Heinrich Bullinger, *Compendium Christianae religionis decem libris comprehensum:* "By holiness we understand that which possesses realities alone, not mixed with their opposites" (*Dilucid.* #453, cited in Heppe, *RD,* p. 92).

8. Mastricht, *Theoretico-practico Theologia* (1714/25) 2.19.8, cited in Heppe, *RD,* p. 93; German and Latin far better in Heppe, *Die Dogmatik der evangelisch-reformierten Kirche,* ed. Ernst Bizer (Neukirchen: Buchhandlung des Erziehungs-vereins, 1935), p. 79 (hereafter *DRK*): "Mastricht (II, xix, 8): Deo *sanctitas* competit (1) non ut accessorium quid, sed ut ipsa *eius essentia;* nec (2) ut aliquid aliunde acceptum; sed ut omnis in omnibus *sanctitatis scaturigo,* Levit 20:8 et 21:15; Ezech. 20:12; 1 Thess. 5:23; nec (3) certa mensura, sed absque mensura *gradu infinito,* quae proin nec augeri nec minui possit, quia ipsa est eius essentia, quamquam declarari magis magisque possit ac debeat, Matth. 6:9; nec (4) ad sanctitatem legis suae aut

In this formulation God's holiness is defined in terms of God as love, act, and being. Put briefly and in our terms, *holiness is the pure simplicity of God's love.* That is exactly the same as saying that *holiness is the dynamic simplicity of God who is love.*

As regards *love,* we must follow the order love-act-being because whatever else is said, God is love. When we say God's being is pure, we mean that the utter simplicity of God is love. We do not just mean that — contrary as this may often agonizingly seem to be — God is loving toward us and the rest of creation (God's proceeding beyond Godself, the *energeia tou theou*), whence we dare to call God love. Rather, we mean that God is love *(essens/esse),* so we know God to be loving. "God is love" is an ontological claim, a claim which merits all the more fierce debate the more its content is examined — but a claim nonetheless about the being of God, indeed about ultimate being. The verb "is" is a present active form of the verb "to be." To be God is to be love. To be

---

cuiuscunque effigiata, sed ut *omnis sanctitatis idea et exemplar ac norma,* 1 Pet. 1:15; Eph. 4:24; nec tam (5) ut particulare quoddam eius attributum; sed ut *universalis affectio, quaevis alia eius attributa afficiens;* nec denique (6) vulgaris quaedam eius *affectio, sed longe praecipua.*" In this section of Mastricht's writings, we have a carrying through to the doctrine of the holiness of God the implications of affirming the various attributes or perfections of God to be expressions of the simplicity of God. For an index of older Reformed dogmatics on this, I am following the leads in Heppe (*DRK,* pp. 54, 55). Most if not all of the older Reformed orthodox theologians agreed that "Deus est *actus purissimus et simplicissimus.*" This teaching is well summarized by Girolamo Zanchius (*De natura Dei* 1) this way: "Liquido apparet, nullam in Deo esse qualitatem seu accidens, quo talis aut talis esse dicatur, sed *sua simplicissima essentia eam esse quidquid est.* Alioquin in Deo dicerem esse aliquid, quod Deus non est . . ." (cited in Heppe, *DRK,* p. 54). Amandus Polanus (*Syntagma theologiae Christianae* 2.7), also cited here in Heppe, elucidates the implications of this teaching (that God is most simple and most pure act), including the reasons for using any language at all for this pure, simple act who is God's being. "(1) Proprietates Dei essentiales sunt *realiter ipsamet Dei essentia;* et nec ab essentia Dei nec inter se reipsa differunt; non ab essentia, quia sic sunt in essentia, ut sint ipsa essentia; non inter se, quia quicquid in Deo est, unum est; a prima autem unitate omnis prorsus differentia omnisque numerus abesse debet. In Deo nihil est, quod non sit aut essentia aut persona." See the rest of this section from Polanus, nos. 2-11; Heppe, *DRK,* pp. 54-55.

ourselves is to be the creaturely reflection of the loving nature or being of God.

In a section on unity and generality in God, Stead notes three ways of considering God as "pure being."[9] One, in line with Aristotle's treatment of substance, conceives of God as "without matter" in the sense of "not belonging to the physical universe" and "having no imperfections or unrealized possibilities," i.e., as "pure form" (or "a pure form"). On this basis God could be considered "a unique particular" — not belonging to a larger class, like substance, and not being one of a series, but still permitting of comparison by analogical — say, biblical metaphorical — language.

Second, God could be described as "pure being" in the sense of "unqualified being," "being itself," or "nothing but being." This view is technically abstract because it presupposes that nothing can be said or thought of God because there is nothing to God that our human reason can comprehend. That is, if there be any referent for "pure being" (or for "God"), it would be "monad," i.e., "the notion of complete absence of content."

Third, "pure being" may be used in the sense of "fullness of perfect being." To take a frail example (mine, not Stead's), one could say that so-and-so is honest (or holy) and mean that he or she either (a) is lacking falsehood (is unfalse) or (b) is true (is truth-full). "It is by making similar assumptions on a higher level of generality that one reaches the position that 'pure being' can be regarded, not just as an abstract term implying a minimum predication, but as an inclusive term implying the sum of all conceivable perfections, whether moral, aesthetical, or metaphysical" (p. 108). Stead calls this "fullness of perfect being. . . . The language in which this mysterious other reality [a reference to Otto's recognition of some people's experience of being encountered with a *mysterium tremendum fascinans*] is described will be extremely various, since the subject tries to categorize it by analogies drawn from other parts of his experience, whether social, aesthetic or philosophical. But it seems

---

9. Stead, pp. 103ff. Page references in the following text are to Stead's *Divine Substance.*

probable that the category of pure being is sometimes drawn upon as a pointer to this type of experience."

Stead does not include "the Holy One" in the representative biblical titles for God which he lists (on p. 167); nor does he, as I wish to do, go on and apply this explicitly to an analysis of what it means to understand God's holiness as "pure being" in the third sense. Whereas "pure being" in the second sense is *nonessentially contentless,* the third sense of "pure being" is *essentially contentfullness.* Perhaps the term for this could be *"metapleroma"* or "suprafullness." It is "incomprehensible" — *aperigraptos,* not contained, not bounded — in the sense that its superabundant fullness cannot be contained by human reason and speech; it is not (as with the second sense) "incomprehensible" because its abstract contentlessness leaves nothing for reason to refer to.[10]

As we shall see in the chapter on the holiness of beauty, there are two sometimes complementary but often fiercely competing tendencies in Reformed (and Cistercian) aesthetics and definitions of "pure" worship. One tends to define purity in terms of absence and elimination and pruning; the other in terms of superabundant presence and grafting on and nurturing. It is not the case that *simplicity* can be assigned, as often happens, exclusively to the eliminating tendency. In fact, the engrafting and nurturing tendency may more serve *simplicity* because the superabundant presence — in this case, of the Holy Other — evokes a response inclusive of all the senses. The one tends to understand simplic-

---

10. On the variety of terms, used of God by Philo and thence passed on to Clement of Alexandria, which have come to be loosely translated "incomprehensible," see Jean Daniélou, *Gospel Message and Hellenistic Culture,* vol. 2 (Philadelphia: Westminster, 1972), pp. 326-27. Daniélou points to this passage from Clement's *Stromata* 5.2.74.4: "Because Moses, as a true gnostic *(gnōstikos),* nowhere encompasses that which cannot be encompassed *(aperilēptos),* he set up no statue in the sanctuary, thus making clear that God is a mystery *(sebasmion),* invisible *(aoraton)* and illimitable *(aperigraphon)."* Daniélou judges *aperilēptos* and *aperigraphos* to be virtually synonymous, and he notes a closely associated word used by Philo and then Clement: *aperinoetos.* The latter I would translate "beyond the limit of reason." That is still very different from a modern common use of "incomprehensible" to mean "unthinkable," the implication being that we cannot know anything about this or that (and surely not about God).

ity as absence of "sensive" (and sensual) distractions. The other tends to understand simplicity as congruence with fullness of the presence of a subject. In the latter the "sensive" (and sensual) accruement is not a distraction but serves to mediate the fullness of relational being. I have used the word "sensive" because I know of no English equivalent of the French *sensible* as that which refers to the senses.

Nor will it do to set "being" off against "becoming," for the one is the presupposition of the other — not a so-called functional alternative to replace a so-called statically ontological option. Eberhard Jüngel is more careful than some of his rapid readers to specify what the title of his book *(Gottes Sein Ist im Werden;* in English, *The Doctrine of the Trinity: God's Being Is in Becoming)* means — and does not mean. The book "is not about a 'God who becomes.' God's being is not identified with God's becoming; rather, God's being is ontologically localized."[11] Far from giving in to the popular illusion that one can do accurate theology minus an ontology of some sort, Jüngel goes on to say, "In theology what is called 'becoming' should be understood ontologically, originally as a Trinitarian category, according to which God does not leave his present state as a past in order to proceed towards a future which is unknown to him, but according to which he is in Trinitarian livingness 'undividedly the beginning, succession and end . . .' (cf. Karl Barth, *Church Dogmatics* II/1, p. 615)."[12]

---

11. Jüngel, p. vii.

12. Jüngel, p. viii. Jüngel acknowledges efforts to avoid a metaphysical argument in his discussion of God's relationality and his intention, whether successful or not, not to think of God only in a functional sense. Jüngel, however, goes on to argue that "The fact that God *becomes manifest* means that God's being is relational being. But if the dilemma sketched above [in an analysis of Gollwitzer's argument] is now to be avoided, if God's being is to be comprehended as *in relation to something* (pros ti [in Greek script]) and yet to be protected from being dependent on every *other thing* (heteron [in Greek script]) without on the other hand the relation becoming the *accidens* of a substance existing in and for itself, then one will have to understand God's being essentially as *double* relational being. This means that God can enter into relationship *(ad extra)* with another being (and just in this relationship his being can exist ontically *without* thereby being ontologically dependent on this other being), because God's being *(ad intra)* is a being related to itself" (p. 99).

When we speak of *"act,"* we mean "the dynamic simplicity of God's being." There are two ways of considering what it means to say God is pure act. One way focuses on completion as ending or cessation of movement; the other way focuses on completeness as perfection of movement of which lesser realities are anticipatory approximations. The first way is suggested when we speak of finality or the final end of things; this is the *finis* at the end of a play — done, finished off, completed. The second way is suggested when we speak of the goal of all things, the ultimate purpose, destination, the telos at which things are aimed, as in the questions "What is the chief end of humans?" and "For what was the world created?" It is in this secondary sense that we most grasp the sense in which we speak of God as pure act, namely, as that transcending end which (or rather, who) draws potential reality forward into actualized reality. It is in this sense that we speak of the living God as the eternally moving mover of all things, in which God's eternally being toward Godself is the presupposition, the prior condition, of God's being in timely and spatially and energetically fashion toward an other, thereby bringing that other into existence.

A classical example of the nuanced relationship between dynamic and static components is Thomas Aquinas's marvelously rich treatment of the being of God within his *Summa theologica*. Incredibly, Aquinas's chief work is referred to by some as an example of a "static" or "rigidly metaphysical" or "closed" (i.e., not "open-ended") system of thought. The judgment, again incredibly, is often accompanied by the explication that it is "Aristotelian." Here the semantic morass becomes so viscous and turgid that terms become almost arbitrary. But if "dynamic" has the central meaning of movement and action, then Aristotle's view of the world is one of the most dynamic ever set forth: the whole is potential moving to actualization. As for Aquinas, the first thing that must be said is that it is his interpretation of the Old and New Testaments which most characterizes him as a catholic theologian and Christian philosopher, closely followed by the traditions, namely, the church's beliefs and worship and ethics and structure which shape that biblical interpretation. When that is recognized, then one can observe that the philosopher on whom Aquinas most drew, who most assisted him philosophically, was indeed Aristotle. The latter's treatment of the movement of potentiality to actualization is at least as dynamic as — no, is far more dynamic than — the alternatives of those who have not thought through the ontological presuppositions of their claimed functionalism.

However, when it comes to his strictest definition of unqualified being, Aquinas chooses a philosophical formulation which — so it seems to me — is not dynamic. There is no movement in the *actus purus,* at least no movement according to the way Aquinas himself describes movement. I think I am correct in this assessment, though I know enough of the range of Saint Thomas's thought not to be surprised by his having somewhere addressed this very objection. The Unmoved Mover is necessary for a universe of movement, and in that sense the divine attribute of immutability is allowed to determine the permissibility and meanings of the other divine attributes, including holiness. Even then, however, when biblical doctrines of God clearly are at irreconcilable odds with Aristotle, Aquinas almost always allows an inconsistency in favor of the biblical material.

The formula that God is the unmoved mover does not sufficiently guard against the presupposition that the greatest reality is nonchange. That presupposition implies that there is such a thing as absolute inertia, unchangeable velocity and direction and energy. The further presupposition is that, even should such absolute inertia be imaginable, it would be possible to make any correlation between that and the biblical analogies for God. Instead of speaking of *the unmoved mover,* it would be more accurate to speak of *the eternally moving mover* if we are to be closer to pointing to the reality upon whom our existence and growth, our forgiveness and new beginnings, our creation and salvation depend. There may or may not be a relatively satisfactory way of expressing philosophically the reality which — rather, the reality who — is pointed to in the scriptures of the Old and New Testaments; but the movement of God's fidelity, the unfolding manifestation of God's steadfastness, the adaptive pursuit of God's loving-kindness, the generation-by-generation constancy of God's covenanting purposes are better served by the conception of God's being eternally moving mover than that of unmoved mover. Steadfastness, constancy, utter reliability, absolute beauty which transforms by drawing the relatively beautiful unto itself are ill expressed by the term and the notion of absolute immutability.

There is something of a continental divide when it comes to thinking and speaking about pure act. For one thing, there is no escaping thinking and speaking about being; ontology can only be procrastinated, but sooner or later the presupposition of existence is wittingly or naively relied upon. For another thing, if one chooses to think of ultimate being as pure act, one still must choose to mean thereby that pure act is nonmovement (completed movement, perfect in the sense of completed) or quintessential movement (eternally continual, infinitely relational, utterly boundless freedom to be together onely) of which all other movements are approximations.

I am aware that language is pulled way out of shape in trying to point to infinitely dynamic being, and I am aware that in making this linguistic attempt one inevitably is thinking and articulating doxologically. That is, language which aims to point in the right direction where ultimately benevolent being is congruently celebrated (and the buffers of qualifications are built into the nature of accurate language in this undertaking) — such language is accurate to the extent that it is also doxological. However, language which knows the impossibility of expressing what is humanly inconceivable is not — is not — just contentless stupor, is not just empty nothingness. Instead, it is superabundantly, overflowingly content-full. The silence is that of awe before the magnitude and beauty of the reality which grasps us. There are normative, canonical guidelines for differentiating between, on the one hand, the pregnant silence of the knowing that we are known by benevolent being and, on the other hand, nihilism of thought and language. That knowing that we are known by benevolent being issues, above all, from the proclamatory story of canonical fidelity as witnessed to in the Scriptures of a scandalously particular instance of human history: the covenanting story of God who is essentially covenanting, who is relationally benevolent by nature. It is to consider this claim further that we turn in the next section.

Covenant and *Perichoresis*

Confessing that God is eternally relational[13] means quite the opposite of what has become known in some circles as a "social doctrine of the Trinity" or, even less guardedly, a "doctrine of the social Trinity." This term — "social Trinity" — has become something of an umbrella under which actually quite different teachings are grouped. One has to distinguish between (a) those who begin with the mystery of God's being the holy other and only turn to analogies drawn from social relations to point to that mystery; (b) those who go a step further and treat social relations as the *imago Dei,* analyzing which we are on safe ground in thinking of and speaking of the Triune; and (c) those who confidently take the ancient terms *hypostasis* and *persona* to mean the same as the modern use of "person" and so actually begin with a description of the human person — not even just the social relation — from which description we know what we mean when we speak of the three persons of the Trinity. The teaching that God is eternally relational sometimes overlaps with the first sense of "social Trinity" — but only with the first, unless it strays into the lapses of the second and third senses. Rather than the rather unguarded use of "social Trinity" which borrows too rashly from the contemporary sense of "person" for the way God is one threely, the use of "communion" is less exposed to the charge of tritheism and yet more appropriately maintains the teaching that God is eternally relational. I find George Sizoulos's work promising in this direction.[14]

13. "Protestant theology cannot formulate the purity of the relationship without an origin of relationship, which as the origin of relationship *is,* in that it *sets itself in relation.* Such setting-itself-in-relation is, understood theologically, pure relationship. And in the sense of such a setting-itself-in-relation God's being is *essentially relational;* God's being is 'pure relationship'" (Jüngel, p. 102).

14. I remain unconvinced about the appropriateness of the term "social Trinity" despite the best efforts to make a case for it, such as can be found in Daniel Migliore, *Faith Seeking Understanding* (Grand Rapids: Eerdmans, 1991), pp. 67-72, and especially in two essays by Cornelius Plantinga, Jr.: "Social Trinity and Tritheism," in *Trinity, Incarnation, and Atonement* (Notre Dame, Ind.: University of Notre Dame

So far in this chapter we have been arguing that all finite forms of being are ultimately and penultimately dependent on infinitely relational being. As eternal love, God's being is dynamic. That statement is redundant, but must be said in order to counter the assumption that there is such a thing as static being. Static being is a contradiction in terms. Now, however, a distinction needs to be pointed out between relational being and relative being. Here again, the use of terms is remarkably fluid; relational and relative being may be understood as overlapping. It can happen that a person can use "relational being" to mean relative, and vice versa. All I can do here is identify what that distinction means as I am using the terms.

To do so I find it helpful to use the language of covenant to describe relational being and to see relative being as intelligible only as a derivation of covenantally understood relational being. There is a Subject being thought and spoken of. The minute one speaks of divine relativity, one is making a comparison between what is divine relativity and what is different from it; one is at least implying interactive response and interactive knowing. Thought and speech in this interactive knowing may

---

Press, 1989), and "Gregory of Nyssa and the Social Analogy of the Trinity," *Thomist* 43 (1986): 33-58. The latter curiously misses the main point of Nyssa's drawing on the relationship between two individual persons like Paul and Peter, which is that they belong to a universal class, thereby arguing for the unity of God when we nonetheless speak of the three *hypostaseis*. Analogies drawn from social relationships can be used, of course; and I am aware that communal analogies are suggested and embraced (covenant is one of them) when I choose to speak of the eternally relational identity of the Holy Triune. However, "social Trinity" as a term comes too packed with modern connotations of "persons" in the plural which are quite different from *hypostaseis* and *personae.* I agree with the familiar warnings on this point registered by such otherwise different theologians as Barth (*CD* I/2, 2nd ed. [Edinburgh: T. & T. Clark, 1975], pp. 348ff.), Tillich (*Systematic Theology,* vol. 3 [Chicago: University of Chicago Press, 1963], pp. 286ff.), and Rahner (*The Trinity* [London: Herder, 1970], pp. 103ff.). Obviously tritheism is far from the minds of those who are comfortable with the use of the term "social Trinity." But the disadvantages of the term far outweigh its dubious utility — especially since already too much of Christian theology has a difficult enough time maintaining its continuity with Old Testament monotheism.

well be, indeed would seem inevitably to be, relative insofar as both (a) the Subject cannot be exhausted by any fixed thought or language and (b) willing interactivity entails the volition to mutual knowability. The known and knowing Subject whose study is the discipline of ontology is covenantal and covenanting by nature. I deliberately use that term "by nature" because I do not want to cashier entirely the terms "essentially" and "really" in the literal sense of *realiter* as that having to do with *res.* Instead, we need to speak of *covenantal ontology,* of fiducial reality, of ultimate relatedness, of the dynamics of relational being, of eternal triunity.

We are bound to use human language whose utility in referring to God partly depends on our recognizing its finitude. The language the church uses to confess the faith is, however, far from arbitrary or a matter of preference. The liturgical, ethical, and doctrinal vocabulary of the church has for its canonical source and refreshment the writings of the Old and New Testaments as interpreted in the successive generations of hope. When we use vocabulary like "love," "holy," "eternal," "being," "essential," we are drawn into an upward-spiraling dialectic in which initial senses of words shape our initial hermeneutics, only to have these initial senses and interpretations judged and corrected to a new level, and so on.

In the following identifying statements of the church or Israel, the indicative implies a reality to indicate: "I am the Lord your God who . . . ," "God is love," "You are my people," "If anyone is in Christ, that person is a new creation," "And the Word was made flesh and dwelt among us full of grace and truth," "The Lord is my shepherd," "I will be who I will be" (or "I am who I am"), "I am the Holy One and you shall be my holy people," "The kingdom of God is at hand," "I will be with you to the end of the age," "Your sins are forgiven you," and so on. The same is true with the vocative and imperative. The following language implies an addresser and an addressee, a questioner and a questioned: "And God said, 'Let there be . . .' and there was . . . ," "Adam, where are you?" "Go, say to Pharaoh . . . ," "Repent and be baptized," "You are the man," "And who do you say that I am?" "Feed my sheep," and so on.

It is my intention here not to be using an "analogy of being" by which to understand covenant, but just the reverse: to define what we mean by being from an "analogy of covenant."[15] Covenant, however, permits a bewildering array of meanings, so once again the focus must be on God's self-disclosure above all through the particularity of that cross on which the eternal Word of God risen from the dead the third day had been killed. The covenant which provides the analogy is that which is worked out — the love which is actualized — through what Calvin calls "the whole course of Christ's obedience."[16] That whole course of Christ's obedience includes the incarnation, learning, ministry, teaching, passion, resurrection, anointing disciples with the Holy Spirit, present activity, and promised coming again. This is summarized in the Pauline description of the Eucharist, when Christ says of the actions he makes with wine: "'This cup is the new covenant in my blood. Do this, as often as you drink it, in remembrance of me.' For as often as you eat this bread and drink the cup, you proclaim the Lord's death until he comes" (1 Cor. 11:25-26 RSV).

Covenanting is the act of promising to give and to receive upon one's word. It is the act of entering an accord with another, the new relationship usually being ratified by some costly exchange of something held in trust. That token or sign of ratification may take a wide variety of forms, like mingling of blood, or eating and drinking together, or exchanging valued persons — as ransom usually. The making of such a binding promise is also usually accompanied by some cultic event during which the benefits of keeping the agreement are extolled and the dreadful woes of breaking the agreement are threatened.

I use the term "analogy" to mean something more specific than sim-

---

15. While I wish to call attention to covenantal analogies, this complements rather than displaces — and in fact, is often expressed in terms of — others, such as the ones Stead, pp. 262-66, calls attention to for pointing to the meaning of *homoousios:* parent-child analogies; the three most used physical analogies (fountain-stream, light source–ray, and vine-branches); human-human relationship; and intrapersonal identity (mind-word). See also J. N. D. Kelly, *Early Christian Doctrine* (New York: Harper and Bros., 1958), pp. 242-47, and Prestige, pp. 107ff.

16. On Jesus Christ as himself the covenant between God and humans, see J. de Senarclens, *Heirs of the Reformation* (Philadelphia: Westminster, 1963), pp. 234-40.

ile or similitude or metaphor. For an analogy functions to say in what respects the things being compared are both alike and unalike. An analogy points to the discontinuities as well as the continuities between the things being compared. Here I am saying that there are certain features common to various ways of establishing a covenant, and that those common features provide an analogy for thinking and speaking of ultimate reality. Moreover, since the scriptures of the Old and New Testaments are canonical for a *theologia crucis,* it is covenantal fidelity of God being counted on in the several covenants, above all the new covenant of Christ's body and blood, which constitutes the analogical material for thinking and speaking of ultimate reality or, which is the same thing, the being of God.

Elsewhere I refer to that as an *analogia assumptionis,* which is a prior step which must be taken in order for trinitarian analogies to work. It is from the specificity of God's love which takes up the human condition and makes it thereby material for redemptive transformation that we can have a solid knowledge of that reality for which an *analogia trinitationis* is an instrument of comparison. Of course — and it should go without saying, except the basics seem to need resaying — the movement from the *analogia crucis* or the *analogia assumptionis* to an *analogia trinitationis* is reciprocal and dialectical, an upward spiral of growth in which the triunity defined by God's self-giving in Christ and the trinitarian understanding of that defining self-giving are mutually corrective and nourishing.

It would be an entirely hypothetical christological analogy to focus either on the person or the work of Christ: for just as we cannot even begin to conceive of the unity of God and humanity in one person apart from the redemptive work of that person, so we cannot even begin to conceive of the work of Christ as redemptive apart from the identity of that unique person in action. Here I am not drawing a parallel between, say, on the one hand, the four Chalcedonian adverbs used to point to the union of the human and divine natures of Christ and, on the other hand, characteristics of the new covenant. Such a parallel indeed merits sustained exploration. Instead I am suggesting a parallel between the unity between Christ's person and his work and the unity between God's steadfast love and its actualization in successive covenantal actions culminating in the new covenant spoken of when Christ says, "This is the new covenant in my blood."

It is difficult not to hear in this saying a reference to the new covenant proclaimed in Jeremiah 31. Difficult or not, Reformed hermeneutics has almost always made that connection because of the way that tradition has viewed the relation between the Old and the New Testaments. That connection does *not* mean a view that somehow Jeremiah predicted that the new covenant he had in mind would be fulfilled in Jesus' death and resurrection. That connection *does,* however, mean that, this side of Jesus' being vindicated by the resurrection as the long-expected Christ, the believing community could not help but see the promise of the new covenant in Jeremiah as being fulfilled in Jesus' saving identity and action.

The fulfillment contains within itself a proclamation that the prior promise is being worked out, actualized, and — equally important — that the fulfillment contains within itself a new promise. Hence the eschatological setting of Paul's account of the Lord's Supper: the showing forth of Christ's death until he comes again. The fulfillment is itself promissory. The promised new actualization of God's steadfast love comes in the form of a new promise, defined definitely by the once-for-all saving person and work of Christ but expanding its universality by the presence and activity of the Holy Spirit.

That is one thing about the relation of the new covenant to the old covenant (which itself was in contrast to its predecessors): old promise actualized in new promise as the story of the unfolding realization of God's steadfast love.

There is another thing, however, about the relation of the new covenant in Christ's blood to its predecessors: the actualization of God's steadfast love in the new covenant is personal in the strictest sense, namely, that God fulfills his own promises in person. Jesus Christ is where promise and actualization are personally united.

Being and act are in him uniquely inseparable; and growth into our respective places in the unfolding narrative of God's steadfast love is growth in the integration of our being and our action, growth in the actions and identity of new creations in Christ. This growth is by the power of the Holy Spirit by whom we are united to Christ and freed to practice our truest — in the image of God created — identity. That is what it means to be transformed daily from one degree of glory to another. "Now the Lord is the Spirit, and where the Spirit of the Lord is, there is freedom. And all of us, with unveiled faces, seeing the glory of the Lord as though reflected in a mirror, are being transformed into the same image from one degree of glory to another; for this comes from the Lord, the Spirit" (2 Cor. 3:17-18 NRSV). We are back — or forward — to Calvin's insistence that the Christ we know is the one united to his body, the church. This is the community of those struggling by the power of the Spirit to live together more and more in conformity with Christ. This community is the context in which analogical thought and language about God's love is actualized in the detailed service of one another after the manner of God's love in action as Jesus Christ to whom we are united by the power of the Holy Spirit.

We are united to the one Mediator Jesus Christ. He is the eternal Word of God incarnate acting redemptively and re-creatively, proclaiming the kingdom of God's presence, going through the cross and resurrection, keeping his promised coming again. The Holy Spirit is the bond — the freeing fetter — by whom we are united to the one mediator and to the many believers. The mediated presence and activity of God in these ways provides the analogical material by which we can think and speak adequately *(Satis est)* about God — and can pray, can talk back to God.

Jesus Christ is the mediator of salvation. This means he is also, at the same time thereby, the mediator of the knowledge of God. That Jesus Christ is the mediator is part of the saving knowledge of God effected by God's self-giving in revelation; but Christ's being mediator is *also the way of God's knowledge of us* and consequently also of our knowledge of God.

There are two aspects of this claim which need more clarification.

The first aspect needs to be stated sharply: salvation and the right knowledge of God are synonymous. This mediated knowledge includes — even mainly consists of — the assumption by the eternal Logos of finite logos, the assumption by infinite Reason of finite reason. It is the continuity of the eternal Word through that which is taken up, that which the eternal Word unites to himself by the power of the Spirit into the one person Jesus Christ, which is the being of God in our midst.

The person of Jesus Christ is *homoousios* with the Father and *homoousios* with humanity. This means that it is in God's movement toward us that we are restored to a right relationship to God, which right relationship includes — or is synonymous with — the redemption of reason. To say the same thing by way of contrast: there is no chain of being except God's being for us in the one mediator Jesus Christ.

The second aspect is that we are known by God in Jesus Christ. He is not just the mediator of our knowledge of God, but is equally the mediator of God's knowledge of us.

This knowledge of us in Christ is not incidental and later, as milliseconds pass in the earliest history of the universe, but is essential to the divine omniscience. From all eternity God knows us through and in Christ. That is to say that the eternal decree is one of elective love. The acceptance is eternally an uncompelled action of the gracious God who chooses us for the loving response of practicing being God's people. That is, God from all eternity calls us into being in Christ, the eternal Word become flesh. We are called to be the interactive recipients of his timely and unrelenting covenantal love going beyond himself, creating and redeeming and sanctifying triunely.

Oh, of course, we inevitably think in terms of priority and derivative; and of course, there is a sense in which God's eternal love exercised in time is a consequence of God's own being eternally love — a consequence of who God is in Godself. But the main point remains: knowledge of us in Christ is not an afterthought occasioned by sin's unexpected arrival on the scene.[17]

17. God accommodates to our finite condition and to our sinful condition. Finitude and sinfulness are not the same thing, sin being in part the distorted use of finitude, and the way we live finitely being much affected by how we face or deny our sinfulness. But God also accommodates to our redeemed condition: we continue to grow in grace, howbeit with much stumbling and struggling, through the ordinary means of grace (hence the term, for which see infra, chap. 6). God's accommoda-

Having said that eternally relational being is covenantal, we can now identify some implications of this for a restatement of the doctrine of *perichoresis*.

In order to define the term as we are using it, I am acknowledging three debatable but, I think, warranted historical judgments. First, A. Grillmeier and others are correct in their judgment that the doctrinal developments through the Council of Chalcedon, in 451, are the logical consequences of the decisions formulated by the Council of Nicaea, in 325. Second, the need to confess the full divinity of the Holy Spirit, corresponding to the confession of the Son's identical being with the Father, called for the development of language more amply to express the mystery of God's being. Third, as used by John of Damascus, perichoretic formulations served that need in his century and culture; and those formulations provide an essential trajectory for sound doctrine ever since.

It was not without struggle that the full divinity of the Holy Spirit came to be confessed and to be received as catholic dogma. Other ways of stating the importance of the Spirit were attractive. Some of these, though stopping short of confessing the full divinity of the Holy Spirit, were true enough as far as they went; and their partial insights became part of the more carefully worked-out adoration of, and speech about, the Spirit.

For example, the Spirit is indeed the Spirit of Jesus. But the Spirit is not the human spirit in this particular man as one might speak of the spiritual side of a man or woman, or speak of spirit as a synonym for a person's soul, or speak of the enduring enthusiasm and inspiring memory of perhaps the world's greatest religious genius.

---

tion is not, in other words, just to remedy sin. Often theologians in the Western Church have too one-sidedly answered Anselm's question *Cur Deus homo?* with Anselm's answer — to remedy sin — and have all too often ignored the tradition of Irenaeus who gave a complementary reason — to be the image toward which humans were created to mature. The incarnation was, according to this tradition, as much for the completion of creation as for the correction of sin. See Gustaf Wingren, *Man and the Incarnation: A Study of the Biblical Theology of Irenaeus* (Philadelphia: Muhlenberg, 1959).

To take another example of an attractive but severely attenuated teaching about the Spirit, it is correct as far as it goes to say that it was by, or in, the power of the Holy Spirit that Jesus did the signs of the kingdom and taught the multitudes and was raised from the dead. But the Holy Spirit does not take the place of the active obedience by the fully human Jesus. The full humanity of the eternal Word made flesh is not Docetized, minimized, or sentimentalized; it is precisely by Christ's taking up and living through the human condition, which emphatically includes testing, that our humanity is healed — as Gregory of Nazianzus rightly insisted.

It is also correct as far as it goes to think of the Holy Spirit as the love which unites the Son and the Father. This is part of Augustine's teaching when he designates the three *personae* as Lover, Loved, and Love. We shall return to this phrasing, as subject to gross misunderstanding as it is, but already here we must note that, more carefully speaking, it is the triune God who is most properly designated Love, and that each of the three ways of God's being one — each *hypostasis* — is Lover, Loved, and Love.

It is ironic — perhaps inherently and graciously humbling — that a term *(perichoresis)* so important to the sound development of the doctrine of God is so difficult to translate. I suspect the difficulty is no accident: it fits the subject matter to which, or whom, it refers, who transcends any formulation but accepts to be thereby sufficiently referred. Sufficient referral means there is enough for wholeness, health, soundness of teaching for the salvation of women and men. One should beware reading too much into the shift from *perichoresis* to *circumincessio* or *circuminsessio,* though it is fertile ground for the imagination to hear a reference to the dance in Greek drama in the literal meaning of *perichoresis:* "procession around."

In any of its forms, the doctrine of the *perichoresis* is the teaching that God's being one is God's eternal relatedness. God's eternal presence threely is God's single being. I choose to use the term "eternal presence" for two reasons: to distinguish it from God's temporal presence, and to lift up "being present" as a fundamental description of what we mean by love. To use an analogy drawn from interpersonal human relations, *we do not so much become present in order to love and be loved as by loving we become present even when part of us is absent. Love is essentially the motion of freedom.*

Location is joyfully serious business. Proximity, tangibility, is highly desirable in every sense of the word — as a faith which confesses the resurrection of the body knows full well. But transcending love incorporates and expresses itself through many forms, including the freedom not to be present in every way. In fact, the *freedom to be present* is essential to the priority of loving presence. Moreover — we are still speaking in terms of analogies drawn from human interpersonal relations — sometimes the most loving presence entails what is experienced as absence. There is such a thing as *loving absence, which, of course, is itself a particular, penultimate form of loving presence.* We have seen this analogy at work when we discussed God's revelation being at the same time God's hiddenness.

In both forms of freedom to be for another, a characteristic of love is to desire the good and the beautiful for the other. This desire is *freely taking delight in the idiosyncrasy of the other* — in what makes a person that person and not some other person. This fundamental respect for the other means honoring and making room for that other person's criteria of the good and the beautiful — lest what is called love be little more than striving to create the other in one's own image. This self-giving and self-discovering desire takes action, and that action arising from desiring the good and the beautiful for another is what is called being of service.[18] The outward motion, the affective movement toward another for the other's — and paradoxically thereby, one's own — integrity, is at the core of what we mean by love if we are to take our clue from the one who washed the feet of his disciples.

In us this helping propensity, this auxiliary drive, is the inevitable expression — no matter how weak or misguided or corrupted — of "being created for," of being created relationally and appetitive and yearn-

18. On the freedom and commitment grounded in God's covenant loyalty, see chapter 5 of Katharine Doob Sakenfeld, *Faithfulness in Action* (Philadelphia: Fortress, 1985).

ing to be present to another and yearning to accept another being present to self. In this respect it is true that humans are created in the image of God, and their knowing ability is exactly this creaturely similitude to God's eternal presence unto self. God's knowability makes room and time for, and is the prior fact of, human knowing — all human knowing, not just the knowledge of God.

To summarize, this chapter restates in what way we can, and must, argue that God is quintessentially dynamic being. Or, put less redundantly, Godself is superabundant, overflowing love which outworks itself in the freedom to be for another, which freedom is the presupposition of the creation of time and space and energy. This is judged to be the case not from changing cosmologies, but because it best accounts for the being which is presupposed in the experience the people of God have of God's covenantal steadfast love culminating in the eternal Word *sarx egeneto,* Jesus Christ, the head of the church, to whom comembers of his body are united by the Holy Spirit.

CHAPTER FOUR

The Purifying Love of the Holy Other

The question now before us is *whether there really is such a thing as creaturely holiness.* To be clear about what this question means, it will be helpful to remind ourselves of where this chapter comes in the structure of this inquiry into the divine attribute or perfection of holiness.

We began with a chapter (1) on the holiness of the cross. That is, as far as Christian theology is concerned, whatever one says about the relation of creaturely holiness to the Holy One is motivated, judged, and quickened by the accomplished fact of the obedience unto death of the one who on the third day was raised from the dead, Jesus the Christ, the Word eternally begotten and also begotten in time with the flesh of the Jewish woman Mary.[1] Chapter 2 pointed to the consequent fact that the social context of this knowledge, this theology of the cross, is the communion of those who belong to Christ, and subordinately to one another, by the power of the Holy Spirit. *Communio sanctorum* has two senses: communion of people and communion of other creatures used by Christ for the gathering, edifying, and mission of those who are united to Christ by the Holy Spirit. The next two chapters deal with the

---

1. For the literature on this, see R. Bernhardt and D. Willis-Watkins, "Theologia Crucis," in *Evangelisches Kirchenlexikon,* ed. E. Fahlbusch et al., vol. 7 (Göttingen: Vandenhoeck & Ruprecht, 1996), cols. 734-36.

ground of this communion of holy people and holy things, namely, the triune being and energy of God. Chapter 3 began with an explanation for treating, first, the holiness of God as pure, simple, eternally relational love, and this chapter (4) treats the holiness of God directed to another as purifying, differentiating, temporally and spatially relational love. In chapter 3 it was argued that an appropriate analogy for God's perichoretic being is the love effective and known from the new covenant of Christ's sacrifice. Now in this chapter we will argue that the differentiation and diversification of God's love toward another result from the undivided acts of the triune God in creating, redeeming, and making holy. The last two chapters deal with only two of the many ways creatures enjoy the benefits of the purifying love of God: delight in the beauty of God's holiness (chap. 5) and the timely hope for holiness of those who are perfectly forgiven (chap. 6).

The Problem of Holiness Posed by Holy Writ

The systematic problem is posed by the canon of the Scriptures, their unity and diversity: Do they all hold good for the church, and if so, how?

Leviticus 19:1-4 provides a sharp summary of the tension which seems to be inherent in what are, for the church, canonical writings: "And the LORD said to Moses, 'Say to all the congregation of the people of Israel, You shall be holy; for I the LORD your God am holy. Every one of you shall revere his mother and his father, and you shall keep my sabbaths: I am the LORD your God. Do not turn to idols or make for yourselves molten gods: I am the LORD your God'" (RSV).

"You shall be holy; for I the LORD your God am holy." This remarkable claim belongs to an immediate literary setting which already goes a long way in shedding light on what is meant by holiness. That is why that single expression cannot be understood except by noting to whom the saying is addressed, through whom it is addressed, and the specificity of the commandments which apply to the congregation of Israel. The specificity of literary setting needs to be kept in mind when pondering some of the other classic passages which have informed the history of Reformed interpretation of holiness.[2]

2. Here are some examples of texts which have been of special importance in the Reformed history of interpretation on holiness (quotes are from RSV):

1 Pet. 2:4-5: "Come to him, to that living stone, rejected by [people] but in God's sight chosen and precious; and like living stones be yourselves built into a spiritual house, to be a holy priesthood, to offer spiritual sacrifices acceptable to God through Jesus Christ."

1 Pet. 2:9-10: "But you are a chosen race, a royal priesthood, a holy nation, God's own people ['a people for his own possession'], that you may declare the wonderful deeds of him who called you out of darkness into his marvelous light. Once you were no people but now you are God's people; once you had not received mercy but now you have received mercy."

1 Cor. 3:16-17: "Do you not know that you are God's temple and that God's Spirit dwells in you? If any one destroys God's temple, God will destroy him. For God's temple is holy, and that temple you are."

2 Cor. 5:13-17: "For if we are beside ourselves, it is for God; if we are in our right mind, it is for you. For the love of Christ controls us, because we are convinced that one has died for all; therefore all have died. And he died for all, that those who live might live no longer for themselves but for him who for their sake died and was raised. From now on, therefore, we regard no one from a human point of view; even though we once regarded Christ from a human point of view, we regard him thus no longer. Therefore, if any one is in Christ, [that person] is a new creation [or creature]; the old has passed away, behold, the new has come."

Isa. 57:13-16: "When you cry out, let your collection of idols deliver you! / The wind will carry them off, / a breath will take them away. / But he who takes refuge in me shall possess the land, / and shall inherit my holy mountain. [Note: Isa. 11:9-10: 'They shall not hurt or destroy in all my holy mountain; / for the earth shall be full of the knowledge of the LORD / as the waters cover the sea. In that day the root of Jesse shall stand as an ensign to the peoples; him shall the nations seek, and his dwellings shall be glorious.'] And it shall be said, / 'Build up, build up, prepare the way, / remove every obstruction from my people's way.' / For thus says the high and lofty One / who inhabits eternity, whose name is Holy: / 'I dwell in the high and holy place, / and also with him who is of a contrite and humble spirit, / to revive the spirit of the humble, / and to revive the heart of the contrite. / For I will not contend for ever, / nor will I always be angry; / for from me proceeds the spirit, / and I have made the breath of life."

Isa. 42:5-10: "Thus says God, the LORD, / who created the heavens and stretched

These passages of Scripture speak about holiness in ways that include two different, perhaps contradictory, perhaps complementary, convictions. The first is that holiness is singular: there is one who is holy, the Holy One, one whose name is Holy, whose glory is not shared with any other. The second is that belonging to the Holy One brings with it the consequence that God's people are holy. Apparently the holy people of God are not just exhorted to be holy; they are assured, at least in the New Testament, that they are holy. If, and this is an ambitious hypothesis, we assume both convictions to be true, the problems posed are: How can God's singular holiness be said to include plural creatures, and how can there be creaturely holiness without implying an increment or unfolding of God's perfection? It may be that the analogies of mirroring or reflecting, of indwelling, of purification, of resonance, and of recapitulation shed light on the relation of creaturely holiness to the Holy One.

Singular and Manifold Holiness

Though the formulation of it may differ from writer to writer, Reformed theologians have usually explicitly or implicitly worked with a distinction between what are called the incommunicable attributes of God and the communicable attributes of God.[3]

---

them out, / who spread forth the earth and what comes from it, / who gives breath to the people upon it / and spirit to those who walk in it: / 'I am the LORD, I have called you in righteousness, / I have taken you by the hand and kept you; / I have given you as a covenant to the people, / a light to the nations, / to open the eyes that are blind, / to bring out the prisoners from the dungeon, / from the prison those who sit in darkness. / I am the LORD, that is my name; / my glory I give to no other, / nor my praise to graven images. / Behold, the former things have come to pass, / and new things I now declare; / before they spring forth / I tell you of them.' / Sing to the LORD a new song, / his praise from the end of the earth!"

3. Heinrich Heppe, *Die Dogmatik der evangelisch-reformierten Kirche,* ed. Ernst Bizer (Neukirchen: Buchhandlung des Erziehungsvereins, 1935), pp. 56ff., and on holiness, esp. pp. 81-86. Cf. Karl Barth, *Die Kirchliche Dogmatik* (Zollikon-Zurich: Evangelisher Verlag, 1932ff.), II/1, para. 29, on the perfections of God.

Before going that far, of course, Reformed theologians traditionally make three things clear regarding human thought and language about the subject of theology, God. First, God's being is the singular mystery whose depths deepen in direct proportion to the growth in the knowledge of God. Second, God is knowable only because God freely chooses to reveal Godself by self-accommodation to the condition of knowing creatures. Third, human thought and language become a sufficient, howbeit both finite and sinful, vehicle of revelation only because God graciously remembers his covenant to make Godself their referent. These three prior considerations mean that the so-called attributes of God are analogically perceived perfections of the Holy One in whom to be love, to be justice, to be freedom, to be holy, and so on are the same thing. The distinction between God's communicable and incommunicable attributes functions among Reformed theologians to attend simultaneously to the plentitude of God's uniqueness and to the reality of God's presence to those who are other than God.

There is not, however, a compelling consensus about which are incommunicable and which are communicable attributes. Holiness appears in both lists, and, it seems to me, for good reason: God alone is holy in that utterly unique holiness which wills and makes room and time for the derivative, subordinate, and declarative holiness of creatures. Eternal love who is God, God's eternal presence to Godself, creates the finite conditions for the extension of that love to another than God: pure love is the fountain[4] of purifying love. It is God who is love as eternal and temporal presence: the infinite freely creates and is present to the finite. The reason the finite becomes freshly, renewably, novelly capable of receiving the presence of the infinite[5] is not that there is a supposed power of reception inherent in the finite. It is because of the continuity of grace, the steadfastness of God to the covenant which is the presupposition of creation, that the finite is continually becoming

4. The imagery of fountain has involved a risk in the direction of panentheism, but is used in the Westminster Confession of Faith, chap. 2, sec. 2: God "alone is the fountain of all being, of whom, through whom, and to whom, are all things."

5. Cf. D. Willis-Watkins, "Finitum Non Capax Infiniti," in *Encyclopedia of the Reformed Faith,* ed. D. McKim (Louisville: Westminster/John Knox, 1992), p. 139.

capable of receiving God's presence. God's love for another is the manifestation[6] — the freely chosen, utterly gracious extension — of pure love who is the Holy One.

So far we have not been speaking of creaturely love — as we shall do in the next section — but only of divine love in its infinitely relational simplicity and in its finitely complex consequence. Creaturely love is the finite response to this eternal love manifest as purifying love of the finite. It is through manifested love that we know God to be eternally love; this eternal love is the same as the hidden depths of the mystery of God's being. Manifested love is the material of our knowledge of God's being behind his gone-forth Word *(ho logos prophorikos)*.

In interpreting the dynamics of manifested divine love, Reformed theologians have given special attention to the covenanting initiative and fidelity of God. By so emphasizing the history of covenants, they claim to be attending to the importance given by the Old and New Testaments to God's covenantal initiative and fidelity. I think they are right in this effort — so long as other complementary motifs in the sweep of biblical material are not thereby discounted.

I should like to add only a footnote to the applicability of this covenantal perspective. I want to claim that the outworking of the new covenant in Jesus Christ — the love of God manifest in the fulfillment of the new covenant in Jesus Christ's person and work — provides the most appropriate analogical material for accurately pointing to the perichoretic being of the Triune. It is good analogical material in the sense

6. On the rich variety of senses of divine presence — and absence — see Samuel Terrien, *The Elusive Presence: The Heart of Biblical Theology* (San Francisco: Harper and Row, 1978), the section entitled "Covenant and Presence in the History of Biblical Religion," pp. 22ff., and especially the notes and bibliography on pp. 50-57. Terrien's argument is that the category of presence is more a key to biblical theology than is covenant. Though I find them to be far more complementary than he does, his main point is quite correct that, after all, it is God's presence — and absence — which is the presupposition of covenantal activity. His concluding chapter, it is important to note, bears the title "Deus Absconditus atque Presens," and this means that at least, as we have noted above, presence and hiddenness are not opposites but in fact: (a) the hidden and the revealed God is the same and (b) we often experience God's presence as not only hidden but as absent. For which see also pp. 320-31.

that it likens two different things by saying in what respects the things being compared are similar *and* in what respects they are dissimilar.

The perichoretic being of God[7] is not a societal event as the fulfillment of the new covenant is, entailing interaction among several persons with discernibly distinct personalities and social roles. I have argued, above, that most so-called social doctrines of the Trinity err by minimizing the dissimilarities between "persons" and what that term is a very poor translation of, i.e., *personae,* already an ambitious translation of *hypostaseis.* The legitimate protests of a *via negativa* have been attenuated by this overfacile translation shift. When we say there are three eternal relations in the Godhead, or better, that God's being is three eternal relations, it does not mean that there are three persons who have an eternal society, fellowship, coming together, growing together. It means that if we are to use "person" in the common manner to refer to a human being, the term more applies to the Holy One than to any of the three ways God is one.

Just as we do not know immediately (unmediatedly), but only from its restoration by the Mediator, the image of God into which humans have been created,[8] so we know the glory of God's being not immediately but mediately as it shines forth in the face of Christ, which shining forth transforms humans from one degree of glory to another. The loving self-emptying for another to fulfill the new covenant, which is the manifestation of God's love in and through Christ and his body, provides a reliable analogy for the eternally steadfast love which is the being of the Holy

---

7. The classic treatment of *perichoresis* is in John of Damascus's *Source of Knowledge (Pēgē Gnōseōs),* pt. 3, "On Orthodox Faith," in Migne, *Patrologia Graeca,* 94:932ff. On the Cappadocians', especially Gregory Nazianzus's and Gregory of Nyssa's, prior teaching, see J. Pelikan, *The Christian Tradition,* vol. 1 (Chicago: University of Chicago Press, 1971), pp. 221-25; G. L. Prestige, *God in Patristic Thought* (London: SPCK, 1952), pp. 236-301, esp. pp. 289-301; and Prestige, "*Perichoreo* and *Perichoresis* in the Fathers," *Journal of Theological Studies* 29 (1928): 242-52. I want also in this note to acknowledge the profitable discussions, in person and in his writings, I have had with James Loder.

8. See Calvin on this knowledge of the original image only from its restoration, in the final edition of the *Institutes* 1.15.4.

One. The *vestigia trinitatis* are not now left in creation itself (a hypothetical case in any event, since the creation Christians know is the theater of God's glorious restoration), but are primarily and reliably discerned in the covenantal love of God outworked in the history of redemption and glorification. The holiness of God is none other than the perichoretic being of eternal Love: pure love as eternal presence of God to Godself, and purifying love as the presence of God to another than God.

Technically this teaching, this method of defining the holiness of God, is not new. Novelty in the doctrine of the Trinity is not a goal to which Reformed theologians passionately aspire. At best, this approach is no more than a proportionately different emphasis on what has been the confession of the one, holy, catholic, and apostolic church. If what is called Reformed theology ceases to be ecumenical, it becomes an elaborate bearing of false witness, a diabolical distortion of truth-saying into chaff on the winnowing floor. The reinterpretation lies rather in a new recovery of the centrality of the attribute of God's holiness in proportion to and in relation to other divine attributes. Thus it is catholic teaching that God is the Holy One whose being, whose glory, whose uniqueness, whose unboundedness, and so forth are identical. However, when different seasons call for different emphases on this or that way of thinking and speaking of God, overcorrections may occur which then in turn require correction. Such a correction is necessary when holiness and mercy, justice and love, freedom and fidelity are thought of as countervalences in a balanced view of God. We experience God's holiness as purifying love. It is precisely purifying because it is love. And it is loving precisely because it is that creaturely purity which God freely wills, freely restores, and freely nurtures in changes which go from one degree of glory to another.

What Is Meant by "Creaturely"?

The icon of the burning bush is an important one in Reformed understandings of the faith, at least according to the interpretation Reformed theologians have traditionally used when treating Exodus 3:1-12. The focus is not so much on the angel of the Lord there said to appear in a flame of fire in the midst of a bush. Rather the focus is on the phenomena that "the bush was burning, yet it was not consumed," and that Moses turned aside to "see this great sight, why the bush is not burnt."

The sign and its function in the narrative belong together. The point is not a theophany per se, astounding as that indeed is. The point is that the theophany signaled the holiness of the calling and the sending of Moses to deliver God's people from bondage in Egypt. There is in this holy encounter a correspondence between the bush's burning without being turned to ashes and Moses' being called and sent by God without being destroyed. We know that Moses got the point because it says, "And Moses hid his face, for he was afraid to see God," and "But Moses said to God, 'Who am I that I should go to Pharaoh, and bring the children of Israel out of Egypt?'"

Aaron is not incidental to the assurance — "But I will be with you" — God gives to Moses. One of the most important aspects of this narrative is that God's appearance, God's call, and God's assured presence do not make Moses into a gold-tongued one, into Chrysostom. In 4:10 Moses is still explaining to God why he is not the person for the job: "But Moses said to the LORD, 'Oh, my Lord, I am not eloquent, either heretofore or since thou hast spoken to thy servant; but I am slow of speech and of tongue'" (RSV). It is Moses the slow of speech and of tongue who becomes, because of God's presence, the instrument through which God delivers his freeing message to Pharaoh. God promises to be the one who always puts God's words into Moses' mouth — and even grants Moses Aaron to speak for Moses the words God puts in Moses' mouth. "Then the LORD said to him [Moses], 'Who has made man's mouth? Who makes him dumb, or deaf, or seeing, or blind? Is it not I, the LORD? Now therefore go, and I will be with your mouth and teach you what you shall speak'" (4:11-12 RSV). God's stubborn economy of grace insists on using Moses as he is, neither minimizing nor romanticizing the servant's inadequacies but turning them to liberating purposes.

Note that these purposes will be vindicated, ratified, by a sign which as far as Moses and the people of Israel are concerned is in their — rather, in God's — future. "[God] said [near the beginning of this particular debate, for there are other debates between God and Moses],

'But I will be with you; and this shall be the sign for you, that I have sent you: when you have brought forth the people out of Egypt, you shall serve God upon this mountain' [Horeb, the mountain of God, 3:1]" (3:12). Mountains of holy ground, as opposed to the high places of the Baalim, loom large in the topography of God's fulfilled promises.

There is a parallel between the interpretation given to the burning bush and the interpretation given to other instances of God's manifestation through creatures. In the next section we will say more about how this interpretation is influenced by Christology, i.e., by one's understanding of Christ as *Deus manifestatus in carne.* Here we need to note how virtually the same interpretation of the burning bush is applied to the creatures' function in the preaching of the Word and the proclamation of the Word through the sacred actions and elements in baptism and the Lord's Supper.

There are serious divisions among branches of the Reformed tradition on this, let alone among Reformed, Lutherans, Roman Catholics, and Eastern Orthodox.

There were and are those Reformed whose preoccupation is above all to avoid the idolatry of attributing to the elements what belongs to God alone. Those who are motivated by this fear do not link as closely as other Reformed theologians, as Bucer and Calvin do, the signs and the reality signified. In fact, much of the liturgy of those of this preoccupation is devoted to warning the congregation against considering the water and bread and wine used in baptism and the Lord's Supper as anything other than ordinary water, bread, and wine. In no sense is there even a consecration of the elements *in usu* in the sense of setting them apart from a common and ordinary use to a sacred use. The congregation *may* be said to be consecrated — but only in the sense that by this act of remembering the significance of Christ's work, the congregation's faith is strengthened and the faithful renew the covenant of which the sacraments are signs. Even so, one must take care — according to this line of thinking — never to confide in the elements, which can easily become, in fact, distractions from the spiritual meaning just as easily comprehended without the elements as with them. "Only believe and you have received" is a favorite dictum for them.

When pushed too far, this tendency in one branch of the Reformed tradition can draw on and reinforce the Docetizing, spiritualizing, and Manicheanizing comfort of those who remain loath to concede that the Word became, of all things, flesh. It is one thing to say that the Word indwelt Jesus, or that the Word became soul or mind or even body — but that *ho logos sarx egeneto* is simply too offensive to be believed.

That is quite a different theology from the one which also insists that the consecrated elements remain ordinary bread and wine and water — but do so for quite a different reason. The consecrated elements remain just bread and wine because it is through the breaking and drinking of them that Christ promised to be present by the power of the Holy Spirit. John 16 is invoked to explain what this means: the ordinary means of grace, preaching and the sacrament (Westminster adds prayer), are just those "media of grace" because they are the appointed ways through which the Spirit takes the things of Christ and applies them to us. If that sounds familiar from elsewhere, remember the title Calvin gives to book 3 of the *Institutes,* which begins with identifying the Holy Spirit as the bond by which we are united to Christ and so enjoy his benefits.

What makes a sacrament is neither the inward reality alone nor the outward sign alone. At just a semantic level this dichotomy would not make sense. "Inner meaning" asks "of what?" and "outward sign" asks "of what?" What makes a sacrament is the connection between the sign and the signified, the link between the creatures of bread and wine and water and the reality *(res).* That link, or bond, is, at least according to Calvin, the Holy Spirit. Baptism is a spiritual washing because of the use the Holy Spirit makes of flowing water outwardly to confirm our belonging to God's people. The Lord's Supper is a "sacred action" because of the use the Holy Spirit makes of ordinary bread and wine, their breaking and pouring and chewing and swallowing, to be the instruments of Christ's presence and consequently of renewed repentance, forgiveness, and walking in newness of life.

What is mainly wrong, according to this realist branch of Reformed sacramentology, with transubstantiation — and with elaboration of so-called consubstantiation developed by those who claimed to be Luther's followers — is *not* the alleged danger of making the elements into idols.

What is wrong with transubstantiation is that, if true, it would forfeit the conditions under which Christ promises to be present, i.e., bread and wine. Calvin's objection to transubstantiation is *not* that it takes the elements too seriously, but that it does not take them seriously enough. Calvin's sacramental realism is just the opposite of a widespread modern Protestant gnosticism for which the elements appear to be nothing more than visual and tactile aids conveniently dispensed with at no cost whatsoever to the nourishment of the congregation. It is more efficient, in fact, to have fewer than more celebrations of the Lord's Supper. And it is far less messy to daub some humidity on the brow of a darling, and dryly quiet, baby than to immerse this member of the elect and to pass her or him, wet and anointed with oil, from thereby rewetted and reoiled member to rewetted and reoiled member of the covenanting congregation.

What the Communication of Properties[9] Means for the Holiness of Humans

Indwelling is often used in the Scriptures for speaking about how God is present to creatures, especially for speaking about God's presence to creatures for the outworking of God's special purpose for God's people.

9. Reformed orthodox theologians distinguished among several senses of the communication of properties in the incarnation (*genus idiomaticum,* according to which the attributes of both natures are ascribed to the one Person; the *genus apotelesmaticum,* according to which the redemptive works of the one Person are ascribed to one of the natures; and *genus majestaticum,* according to which the human nature is magnified by the properties of the divine nature). Reformed theologians usually held to the first two kinds of communication of properties, but not to the *genus majestaticum,* which they felt compromised, by the doctrine of the *bodily ubiquity* (not just ubiquity, to which every party held, but bodily ubiquity), Christ's full humanity. See "Ubiquity," in *Encyclopedia of the Reformed Faith,* pp. 378-79. Note the prominence given the *koinōnia idiōmatōn* in Cyril of Alexandria's debates with Nestorianism, e.g., his treatment of the fire and coals of Isa. 6:6. Cf. Pelikan, 1:242-52, and Rouët de Journel, ed., *Enchiridion Patristicum* (Barcelona: Herder, 1959), pp. 646-55.

The prologue to John's Gospel points to a unique kind of dwelling which is becoming: the Word became flesh and dwelt among us full of grace and truth. . . . The Word is that by which all things were created. Special reference is made to humans, in whom the Word is the light that lightens them all. This generally present Word is present in a unique way in Jesus the Jewish Messiah, the one not received by those he came to save.

Now the specialness of this indwelling that is becoming flesh is not, so far as I can tell, spelled out in John's Gospel. But the revolutionary, uprooting and replanting, claim that Jesus is the Word made flesh dwelling with us full of grace and truth — this claim was so startling, and offensive, that it set in motion the doctrines of God and concomitant Christologies developed especially in the period from Athanasius through the Council of Chalcedon.

The biggest decision from which subsequent issues were debated was the one of the doctrine of God: Does the doctrine of God include of necessity Christology and pneumatology and a redefinition of the relation of redemption and creation? It would have been a tremendous relief — and that is still the appeal of genuine Arianism — to settle on a view of God as being so utterly transcendent as not to be able, by definition, to touch or be touched by creation, let alone by sin. There was a good reason for the remarkable tenacity of Arianism well beyond the conciliar, and imperial, decision against it. Arianism, ancient and modern, offers a satisfying way of accounting for that large part of the biblical messages which seems to be aimed at so distinguishing God from creation as to make any real (*res,* "reality") connection unthinkable, blasphemous. There is great prudence in keeping a safe distance from God. There is a kind of comfort in believing that, while Godself may be behind divine manifestations, God by definition cannot be directly related to creation.

Hence Arius's reading of the Mediator: Jesus Christ is between the being of God and creaturely existence — the Mediator's being is like God's being, indeed none is as like God as the Mediator, but is not of the very same being as God. For the very same reason, mediation by a third party (or to use analogy not easily found in what survives of

Arius's thought, a gear between wheels of different sizes and speeds, or a transformer transferring energy between two currents of different voltage), the Mediator could not be of the very same being with human beings and still be the necessary Mediator.

In combating this extremely persuasive guarding of the boundaries between God and creation, Athanasius drew on a rich variety of images. It is the combination of three of them that is of special interest for understanding that particular indwelling which is becoming.

The first one we have already noted, the burning bush. Athanasius anticipates some later Christological developments. Perhaps it is more accurate to say that developments up through the Council of Chalcedon were nuanced elaborations of Athanasius's central teaching. The context for this comparison — burning bush and person of Christ — is the discussion of what happens to the humanity of Jesus in the incarnation of the eternal Word *homoousios* with the Father.

He, Jesus Christ, is like the burning bush in this respect: the human nature of Christ is no more destroyed by the incarnation than the bush was consumed by the fire of God's holiness; and the ground is holy, but it remains solid ground on which one who is called may walk with shoes removed since the ground is said to be, and thereby is, holy. The ground and the bush are holy because of the presence of the Holy One; the one who is present does not get holy because he or she comes into an already holy place. What makes the humanity holy is the union of the eternal Word with the flesh.

The second image is that of the ruler who returns to take back the territory and the society which belonged to him always but which an interloper sought to take over and keep. The incarnation can just as well be called the inpolisation, insocietation: the entry of the Lord into the city and the restoration of humanity, including the restoration of reason, which is a large part of salvation to all those in whom the light has shown but who have not recognized him nor received him. This, incidentally, is a good example of why Aulen's typology, set forth in the volume *Christus Victor,* is helpful only up to a point rather quickly arrived at: all three types, plus others, like the healer, are intertwined in Athanasius's account of the atonement.

A third image informs the other two — or at least is so much a part of the other two that we cannot understand Athanasius's thought unless we get this one straight. It is that the eternal Word contains all things and is contained by none.[10] This teaching of Athanasius is sometimes described as his not having "a container view of space."[11] However, it may be more accurate to say that his way of putting the matter entails a radical shift of perspective on space, a paradigm shift which both redefines space and — so to speak — relocates space. It "relocates space" in the sense that the including subject and the included object are switched from the way divine indwelling is often considered. There is indeed such a reality as *sacred space,* but it is *inclusive holiness,* whereas the bush (or mountain, temple, tabernacle, congregation, element, breaking, or pouring) is *included holiness.* They are holy only as a manifestation of the inclusive holiness.

Here we need to acknowledge two extremely attractive alternatives which make moot the question about the communication of the attribute of holiness to creatures. Both are obvious: pantheism and one kind of panentheism.

The first holds the view that everything is god, this everything being called "world" just as well as "god" since they are ultimately the same. There does not have to be a communication of properties from one to the other: there is only the one god-world, world-god.

The kind of panentheism which obviates the problem of the communication of properties holds the view that god is, of necessity to god's

---

10. "For he [the eternal Word] was not, as might be imagined, circumscribed in the body, nor, while present in the body, was he absent elsewhere; nor, while he moved the body, was the universe left void of his working and providence; but, thing most marvelous, Word as he was, far from being contained by anything, he rather contained all things himself; and . . . while present in the whole of creation, he was at once distinct in being from the universe, and present in all things by his own power" (Athanasius, *On the Incarnation* 17, but see also 20-23, in which Athanasius beautifully portrays the intertwining of the person of Christ and the work of Christ, in E. R. Hardy, ed., *Christology of the Later Fathers* [Philadelphia: Westminster, 1954], pp. 70-78).

11. See the companion volumes by T. F. Torrance, *Space, Time, and the Incarnation* (London: Oxford University Press, 1969) and *Space, Time, and the Resurrection* (Grand Rapids: Eerdmans, 1976).

being, in everything in such a way that there is a remainder which is not in another. Everything is holy because everything has something of god in it, but there remains a holiness not used up by, not just the sum total of, the divine presence in everything.

This kind of panentheism is a popular way of holding together what is popularly called god's — or the gods' — immanence and what is popularly called god's — or the gods' — transcendence. (I suppose one must mention a crude variation of this kind of panentheism — crude because it is not even consistently panentheistic but ironically becomes a form of dualism. I mean the aweless practice of speaking about "the immanent god" and "the transcendent god.") This (not its crudely dualistic variation) kind of panentheism presupposes an unbroken chain of being. More being is at the top, and there is lesser specific density of being (or cooler being, as with the soul), as it were, the more one moves down the descending levels of existence. This chain of being, more purely divine at one level and less purely divine at other levels, is attenuated but never broken. It is inherent to the continuity of god's being and to the creature's being, quite apart from the novelty of grace and the continuity of God's steadfast love efficacious and therefore known from the way God makes and keeps his covenantal promises.

If Reformed theologians ever use language that is resonant of a chain of being, they are predictably clear about two things: that such a so-called chain of being is mainly broken not by degrees of finitude but by sin; and that the continuity of reality is the chain (recall Calvin's *Institutes* 3.1.1, the bond which is the Holy Spirit) of becoming, by grace alone, new beings in Christ. This *chain of new being* means the forgiveness of sins for the sake of the one who took the best of the old to the cross and tomb and sprang the gates of hell. That is, costly reconciliation is the presupposition of new being. The accomplished forgiveness, for Christ's sake alone, engages people in the church militant in the fight against injustice, against falseness, against sin and sins.

By sin I mean all that is off the mark of what God intends, all that is counter to the hidden mystery revealed in Christ for the whole of creation. Sin is the willful or naive choice of death over life, a choice barely known to us when our need for denial has reduced the conscience to a tiny ember. Sin is the weighting (the "weight of sins which so closely presses") of death over life, the election of nothingness over the fullness of love, the seeking ultimate delight in what leaves us starved and bored to death. All these forms of sin are the rejection, by omission perhaps even more than by commission, of the good news of the law whose purpose is the blessed holiness willed for creatures by the God known and efficacious in Christ.

Sin is humans' (forget about the angels for the moment) choice to be separated from God, a choice which God's sovereign love does not permit from God's side. Our sin may make us try to live out the illusion of being separated from God, may make us confuse our projected alienation from God with God's supposed alienation from us, may make us equate our experiences of the wrath of God with divine rejection rather than see the unrelenting unfolding of God's benevolence against our stubborn self-destructiveness and other-destructiveness.

Athanasius's view — that the Word by whom all things are made contains all things and is contained by none — does indeed admit a rather specific imagery of what *might be called* dynamic, grace-filling panentheism. There *can* be a very particular kind of panentheism — but *only* in the sense that all things are in God and God can be said to be in them only because they participate in the larger reality from which they come, in whom they live and move and have their being, and toward whom they all tend. For example, the saints are said to be filled with the Holy Spirit because they are caught up in the larger reality. This experience is somewhat like a person who has been swept off his or her feet in the spring rush of the Merced River. That person has some, often an overwhelming amount, of the Merced River in him or her. The larger, inclusive reality is partially included in, is partly within, the nearly drowned person! When extended to baptism, this simile means being caught up in the coming of the Holy Spirit, sweeping people off their old secure footing and ground, being filled with the larger, inclusive reality, and in that way indwelt by the Spirit who is not thereby contained. The connection of death and rebirth is not incidental to baptism imagery and gasping for new air to fill the lungs after thrice being immersed. Nor is the connection between the Holy Spirit and fire, the *pur* of purification: being caught in this fire is costly refinement, the vaporizing of the dross of sin. It is — to switch to organic imagery — the pruning of the vine, the daily mortification and vivification.

We belong to a larger reality, are possessed by a larger reality, come to find ourselves as ones whose identity is our belonging together to an infinitely loving reality. It is belonging to another, finding ourselves in God's loving purposes, discovering the coexistence of creatures who belong to Christ and to each other and then also to self. This belonging to a larger reality of love, this finding oneself in relation to an other within this larger reality, is by grace alone through faith. That is, it is not an inherent condition of creation or of the nature of the Creator. It is an utterly free gift of the including one to include the included. The way of this including the sinner is forgiveness for Christ's sake. This is the direction and dynamic of the finite indwelling the infinite, of the not-yet-perfectly-holy indwelling the eternally Holy One.

This is also what is behind the language of the taking up, the assumption, of the flesh by the infinite Word. The question is not how it is possible for the infinite to be included in the finite, or for God to be included in human nature, or for Christ to be in the bread and wine. The question is, what does the accomplished fact mean for us and our salvation and for the outworking of God's love for the whole of creation? To what end did the eternal and boundlessly Holy One take up the total human condition, sin excepted, so that it, united with the eternal Word, experiences the judgment, death, resurrection, and life of hope in Christ the incarnate eternal Word crucified, dead, and buried, third-day risen, presently active head of his body, and coming-again Lord? This theology of the assumption by the Word is the underlying image in interpreting the parable of the prodigal son as the whole presence and action of reconciliation in volume IV of Barth's dogmatics. One does not grasp the whole sweep of reconciliation depicted in this volume if one minimizes the image of the taking up of the condition of the included covenant partner by the including One who is the initiator and fulfiller of the covenant.

In Protestant orthodoxy, as we have seen, distinctions were made among different kinds of communication of divine and human properties in the incarnation. As we have noted above, one of the questions asked was whether or not holiness is a communicable attribute of God. If one says no, there is no basis for calling people to holy lives, no reason to call the rapscallion congregation at Corinth "saints." If one says yes, then one has to consider there to be a unique holiness that does not destroy, bypass, denigrate the other-than-God-ness, the createdness, of the ones made holy by the unmade Holy One. For this consideration the images of fire and light, of death and rebirth, and of Word and words may afford some viable ways of thinking about the nature of the one holiness and the nature of the manifestations of this one holiness.

We can turn now to say something of the reality brought about by the communication of the property of holiness to the creature, *by which communication the creature is said — declared — by God into being holy.* We are now speaking not of the communication of properties in the person of Christ, i.e., the hypostatic union of two natures in Christ. We are now speaking of that kind of unity effected by the Holy Spirit, who binds us to Christ and to the other members of his body. This deals with the communication of Christ's holiness to the members of his body, and even *in usu* to other components of the *communio sanctorum.*

As I write this, I can see no way around speaking of being, of *res,* after which reality is named. Perhaps it is best to speak of ultimate reality instead of being, and there may be other circumlocutions which do not set off alarms of "static" and "abstractly metaphysical"[12] and "nonrelational" which the use of "being" frequently sets off. At any rate, I do not know of, nor can I conceive of, anything such as "static being." Those two terms cancel each other out.

To be is corelational life, revealed hiddenness eternally as God, hidden manifestness as relational to God: perfect being and perfect being in relation to another than God. Creaturely existence is the other-than-God's ultimate dependence on being itself, *"a becoming which is being*

---

12. For an accurate evaluation of the sense in which Barth's work at the time was "antimetaphysical" yet is a way to permit him to discuss matters traditionally assigned to "metaphysics," see B. McCormack, *Karl Barth's Critically Realistic Dialectical Theology: Its Genesis and Development, 1909-1936* (Oxford: Clarendon, 1995), pp. 245ff.

Godward." I take these following to be, "for all practical purposes" (literally: *praxeis tōn apostolōn*), references to the same reality: new being in Christ; being filled with the Holy Spirit; being baptized into Christ's death and resurrection so as to walk in newness of life; remembering which proclaims Christ's death until he comes again; for Christ's sake being convicted of sin and for Christ's sake being assured of forgiveness; freedom to practice the essentials of the covenant and freedom from confusing essentials with indifferent matters.

I want to designate this a *covenantal ontology* because: (a) it is justly relational, and (b) its relationality is that of a loving, just promise to the creature being fulfilled.[13] The grace-filled creature is becoming to have a future. One may also — I want to — designate this a *declarative ontology* because being said by God into being new is exactly the content of the restoration of the image of God into which, and toward which, humans are created. God's word effects that which God purposes and speaks. "God said, 'Let there be . . . ,' and there was. . . ." Forensic justification is not what we get instead of ontological justification: the only way of ontological justification (if one chooses to buy into the language of such an implied false dichotomy in the first place) is declarative justification for Christ's sake alone. *Such declarative, covenantal ontology needs to correct and inform and redefine whatever else is meant by ontology*

---

13. An "actualist" ontology, at least as B. McCormack contends Barth uses, is, as far as I can tell, quite close to what I mean by covenantal ontology in this quote: "Bonhoeffer was right about one thing; Barth had indeed said good-bye to all metaphysically based religion. But at no point did he simply fall back on the biblical or creedal language as an unimpeachable *given* and say 'take it or leave it.' What he did, instead, was to elaborate a non-metaphysical, actualistic (divine and human) ontology which took the place of the classical metaphysics of being and the modern metaphysics of the religious a priori and which completed that language and made it meaningful in a new and different way" (from an unpublished paper entitled "Beyond Nonfoundational and Postmodern Readings of Barth: Critically Realistic Dialectical Theology," p. 32). My own hesitation with the word "actualist" is that I do not think it sufficiently escapes what is here called classical metaphysics. For at least in the case of Aquinas, reality is the actualization of potential — and this, Aquinas's, ontology is "dynamic" in the sense that reality is the movement from potential to actual, God being equated by him, Aquinas, with the unmoved mover.

— but surely we need to be well beyond posing the question in terms of ontological versus forensic transformation.

To the question "Can creatures really be holy, or are they just said to be holy?" the accurate shorthand answer is "Creatures can really be holy because by God they are said to be holy." This creaturely holiness is the work of God's word which is efficacious declaration. The Word "calls into being holy" what was not but what God elects to become holy. The ontology of being new in Christ is Word event, holiness is declarative reality, the new being is like the original creation only more so — having a glorious being because of the efficacity of the Word. Creation is rightly read from the experience of new creation. The image of God in which we are created is savingly known only from its restoration. "For what we preach is not ourselves but Jesus Christ as Lord, with ourselves as servants for Jesus' sake. For it is the God who said, 'Let light shine out of darkness,' who has shown in our hearts [or, illuminated our hearts, turned on light in our hearts: *elampsen, illuxit*] to give the light [*pros phōtismon, ad illuminationem*] of the knowledge of God in the face of Christ" (2 Cor. 4:5-6 RSV).

Is this creaturely holiness just (!) a duplication of God's holiness or an uninterrupted extension of God's very own holiness? Neither. Just as the creature is another than God, the creaturely holiness, communicated holiness, is another than the Holy One's holiness — uncommunicated holiness. To say more about this kind of creaturely holiness, we need some light on the matter. I mean that *declarative or covenantal ontology is also reflective or splendorous ontology.* Word and light are often used to point to the same reality. We find this in the prologue to John's Gospel. We see it dramatically in the narrative of John 9: hearing the Word is equated with seeing the light, and the man born blind is made to see by the one he only later sees to have been his healer.

Let me say in passing that it is worth noting the intricate way Flannery O'Connor deals with light, darkness, seeing which is not seeing, and blindness which is seeing in *Wise Blood* and in the short story "Revelation." Or again, see and hear (seeing and hearing cannot be separated since hymnic praise triggers a certain vivid inward sight, perhaps particularly acute in those of limited physical sight) the *Phōs Hilaron* and

"Immortal, Invisible, God Only Wise," in which the revealing light is also a hiding light.

What substance, reality, thereness, and hereness has this creaturely holiness? That of reflection and resonance. It is reflected holiness, as when a mirror gives back patterns of light, a splendid image of that which is reflected. Thus we have in 2 Corinthians that we are being changed from one degree of glory to another and the Spirit causes us to reflect the image of God who is Jesus Christ, the one in whose face we see the glory of God and we ourselves are given faces which shine back the light in the face of Christ Jesus. It is also resonant holiness as answering back God's calling. The Word-Light calls and evokes respondability (as *Verantwortlichkeit* is a variation of the German "to answer"). This extends to the scandal of God's calling humans to speak God's Word: by God's effective calling, preaching of the Word is really one form of the very Word of God. There is no hint, according to the Reformed tradition, that a creature becomes inherently holy by the sacrament of ordination to ministry of the Word proclaimed through preaching and sacraments and discipline. But there is no mistaking the fact that God's calling and gifting mean that a person is used to speak God's Word humanly. *"Praedicatio verbi, verbum Dei est."*

This reflective, resonant holiness of the creature is imperfect. There is growth in creaturely holiness as creatures are drawn forward to perfect holiness. That growth in holiness is maturation in the practice of being perfectly forgiven. This perfect forgiveness is what makes sinners fit ambassadors of the costly reconciliation elected by God in Christ. Creaturely holiness is rich participation in the *communio sanctorum,* a hope-full life together. Which hope? The sure hope of the resurrection, that resurrection which includes the body. Yes, of course, holiness is an eschatological category — as is the whole of the Christian life — so long as we mean by "last things" the end times which have already broken in on us. These end times are a *fait accompli* in which we are graciously and freely caught up. This hope is active in good works which themselves become holy by God's loving acceptance of them for Christ's sake. This means that, at least in the Reformed tradition, we hope in such a way that we are freed for the third use of the law, to constrain and expose and guide and enliven those whom God has called into being God's people.

What the Communication of Properties Means for the Humanity of the Holy One

Now the most difficult question is posed: whether or not creaturely holiness has any effect on the holiness of God.

I confess to be stymied on this one. I suppose I am an agnostic on this issue in the technical sense that I do not know. I remember Augustine's retractions and his observation that one of the most important theological terms is "I do not know." Yet I think one must venture a provisional decision which may well be an implication of what we have argued about the *including and the included forms of holiness.* Remembering my baptism and not doubting that even Reformed theologians are covered by the garment of Christ's righteousness, I shall dare asserting the relevance of five observations for this most difficult question.

First, there is always the definition of terms used both in the form of the question and in any essayed reply. In this case the key term is "effect": Does creaturely holiness have any effect on God? When I pose that question, I mean by "effect" an influence on God's eternally being love (or — which is the same thing — on the eternal way of God's being love). By "effect" I also mean a motion which moves God's eternal being and an action which makes God more perfect than God would be without it.

When "effect" is used in these senses, then, as far as I can tell right now, the answer must be: "No. Creaturely holiness does not have an effect on God's being eternal unto Godself."

On this point it may be helpful to note that there are different senses of "change" when considering the divine attribute of immutability, as noted by Stead in referring to Rouet de Journal's organization of doctrinal headings: ". . . *unicus, simplex, immutabilis.* There is only one God (though no doubt his influence may be conferred upon, and found in, other beings); he is undivided (for if one finds in him distinctions of powers, or persons, these are not thought to infringe his wholeness or 'simplicity'); and he is not subject to change (at least, not to moral change, nor to change imposed from without, though he may in some sense respond to changing human needs)." If a person decides — as is very often done — that by definition "substance" is unchanging, then, again, by definition a so-called static ontology would be implied. But it is Stead's judgment that "the notion that if God is a substance, he must be an unchanging substance is, I think, a mere product of association. . . . But of course, God can be, and has been, represented as a changing substance, and indeed as one that is ever-changing and infinitely adaptable."[14]

However, if the question is asked whether creaturely holiness has any effect on God's being unto another, on God's being *ad extra* — if the question is asked whether creaturely purification has any effect on God's purifying love — then, as far as I can tell right now, the answer must be: "Yes. The limited autonomy which comes to creatures by God's self-limiting, self-accommodating love for another means that *God is really* (res, realiter) *being compassionate in the outworking of his covenanting purposes for another.*"

It seems fruitlessly circuitous to speak of God's love in a way that excludes divine passion, and by that I mean passion experienced by God. At the very least, one would have to admit a radically redefined use of passion by arguing that analogical language about God tells us as much what cannot be said about God as what can. William Placher is correct;[15] and in this Placher quite rightly accords with Eberhard Jüngel and Jürgen Moltmann when he observes that it is not sufficient to have recourse to a rhetorical (my term, not Placher's) understanding — the one sometimes used by some Reformed theologians — of the *communicatio idiomatum* to protect, as it were, God's nature from passion.

14. Christopher Stead, *Divine Substance* (Oxford: Clarendon, 1977), p. 188. Stead refers to his study, pp. 106 and 171.

15. William C. Placher, "The Vulnerability of God," in *Toward the Future of Reformed Theology*, ed. D. Willis and M. Welker (Grand Rapids: Eerdmans, 1999), pp. 192-205, esp., on this point, pp. 202-3.

On this point I would only add that another use (a so-called more ontological than rhetorical use) of the doctrine of *communicatio idiomatum* not uncommon in Lutheran orthodoxy served mainly to provide for the communication of divine properties (e.g., ubiquity) to the human nature, not so much the other way round (and not with human nature's ability to suffer).

Barth's little essay "The Humanity of God" is, as he makes it clear he wants it understood to be, a genuine turning around of his earlier turning around, a correction of the earlier correction he had to make against the anthropologizing habit of much of nineteenth-century theology. Barth's earlier correction[16] was to make clear that "God is not man in a loud voice." Barth's subsequent correction is *not to deny* or reverse the first but *to expand even further the meaning of the incarnation* for our language and thought about God.

It seems to me that part of what it means to recognize the authority of Scripture being God's written Word *pro nobis* is the cultural relativity its human authenticity entails. Take narratives rife with anthropomorphisms. Rather than being seen as belonging to the richness of multilayered meanings of biblical materials, they are often squeamishly filtered out in a misguided so-called purifying enterprise. In fact, however, they may well be considered symbolic in the way Tillich uses that term to mean that which participates in the reality to which it points — provided one sees that anthropomorphisms often function "by contrary" to point to what God is *not* like, i.e., often function "by accommodation" as material of a symbolic *via negativa*. An example of this would be the contrast between the depiction of God who rejects Saul because, as the account goes, he does not obey God's order to slay all the enemy army and the depiction of God embodied who forgives those who slay him as a blasphemer and seditionary. On this, as on other a priori definitions of God, the cross of the risen Lord provides the primary criteria which define what God we are talking about.

One way of putting this answer is to affirm that calling on God,

16. Nicely summarized in the chapters of *The Word of God and the Word of Man* (New York: Harper and Bros., 1957).

prayer as one of the creature's chief acts of faith, is heard, accepted, acted upon by God. This applies especially to that fundamental prayer which cries that God's will and not ours be done. The whole covenantal history depends on, presupposes, acknowledges the fact that the God witnessed to by the scriptures of the Old and New Testaments hears the cries of his people and is moved to acts of deliverance.

Second, eternally relational being which is love pure and simple is ultimate reality. Purifying love is toward another than God and includes the creature. That love of God toward another includes the response of the creature, which above all entails participating in the loving covenantal fidelity of God which engenders repentance and newness of life in Christ. There is a concentricity of God's love: the eternally being unto Godself, the conditioned and accommodated being of God for another, and the consecrated creaturely being for God and for the rest of creation.

When I say God's holiness is affected by creaturely holiness, I mean it in the second and third senses. But when it comes to God's relational simplicity, I think we must maintain that God's perfection is not augmented, made "more perfect" (!) by creation. Creation comes about, is, befalls, so that there is another than God. All this is the doing of eternal love which, not out of want but out of perfection, wills to share that covenanting identity, singular love, with another. Only in this way, it seems to me, can we hold together revelation and the selfhood of God; that is, revelation is not just revelation of revelation of revelation, but revelation of Godself.

Third, when I use the words "eternal" and "eternity" and "eternally," I do not mean that which time replaced and which shall at the end of time be restored. Time is not the time-out of the eternal. Time is not some putting on hold, some cessation, of eternity to make room and duration for creation and redemption to happen. Eternity is, so to speak, equidistant and equispatial and equienergetic. That means that a spatial geography or cosmography, in which we finite and sinful and forgiven creatures think and speak, is the context of our conditioned, contingent response to the mystery of eternal love who is God triunely. God's own being unto Godself is adored and praised by words, thought, actions which are trustworthy pointers to the mystery but never substitutes for it. The eternal holiness of God encompasses its lesser manifestations.

Fourth, the communication of properties is not to be confused with what Calvin, and others, calls the "wonderful exchange."[17] The wondrous exchange refers to the way what is Christ's becomes also ours. It refers to our condition when the eternal Son has taken on the human condition. The benefits of Christ's being mediator apply to us since we are members of Christ's body by the power of the Holy Spirit — that Spirit, *nota bene,* which is never without the Word. These are the effects on us of the active obedience of the unique hypostatic union of humanity (Mary's humanity, and therefore her timely Son's humanity) and the eternal Word.

Fifth, the *communicatio idiomatum* is unilateral. The human properties are not communicated to the divine, no matter how true it is that we

---

17. "Since, however, this mystery of Christ's secret union with the devout is by nature incomprehensible, he shows its figure and image in visible signs best adapted to our small capacity. . . . Godly souls can gather great assurance and delight from this Sacrament; in it they have a witness of our growth into one body with Christ such that whatever is his may be called ours. As a consequence, we may dare assure ourselves that eternal life, of which he is the heir, is ours; and that the Kingdom of Heaven, into which he has already entered, can no more be cut off from us than from him; again, that we cannot be condemned for our sins, from whose guilt he has absolved us, since he willed to take them upon himself as if they were his own. This is the wonderful exchange, which he out of his measureless benevolence has made with us; that, becoming Son of man with us, he has made us sons of God with him; that, by his descent to earth, he has prepared an ascent to heaven for us; that, by taking on our mortality, he has conferred his immortality on us; that, accepting our weakness, he has strengthened us by his power; that receiving our poverty unto himself, he has transferred his wealth to us; that, taking the weight of our iniquity upon himself (which oppressed us), he has clothed us with his righteousness" (Calvin, *Institutes* 4.17.1, 2, ed. J. T. McNeill, trans. F. L. Battles, 2 vols., Library of Christian Classics, vol. 21 [Philadelphia: Westminster, 1960], pp. 1361-62). On the function of *accommodatio* in Calvin's theology, see D. Wright, "Calvin's 'Accommodation' Revisited," in *Calvin as Exegete,* ed. P. De Klerk (Grand Rapids: Calvin Study Society, 1995), pp. 171-90. On the various ways Calvin uses "poverty," see Bonnie L. Goding Pattison, "The Concept of Poverty in Calvin's Christology and Its Influence on His Doctrine of the Christian Life and the Church" (Ph.D. diss., Princeton Theological Seminary, 1997).

can properly think and speak of God only when our starting point is God manifest in the flesh. That is, by virtue of the incarnation God does not cease to be infinite, perfectly holy, perfectly knowing, almighty, all-merciful, in short, the Holy One. The infinite holiness of God encompasses, includes, its timely and spatial and energetic manifestations.

CHAPTER FIVE

The Holiness of Beauty

What is the chief end of man?
To glorify God and enjoy him forever.

This opening of the *Shorter Westminster Catechism* contains the components of the issues dealt with in this chapter. In it we will treat two closely related questions: *whether what we call beautiful is a penultimate intimation of the glory of God,* and *whether God's rule over the microcosm is primarily through conversion of delight mediated through the structures of justice.* When we recognize that an essential aspect of holiness is beauty, we have a better angle from which to reconsider definitions frequently given to the glory of God and the sovereignty of God, and from which to understand something of the awe-filled love which this beauty inspires.

We have just considered the nature of purifying love, and we now are considering one form of this purifying love. Sacred beauty is the superabundance of purifying love, precedentially glorious in the eye of the beholding Creator and consequentially delightful in the eye of the beholding creature. Put differently, *beauty abounds as a form of the accommodated glory of God which evokes an astonished recognition of the congruence between the reality of a thing and its expression. The super-*

abundance of purifying love is that to which something called beautiful is diversely fitting, congruent, proportional, or apt. Diversity is not accidental to beauty anymore than, to use the boldest of analogies, the eternal relations are accidental to the unity of God. Beauty as accommodated glory is naturally polymorphic, polytonic, polychromatic, polyrhythmic, polydelectable, polysensual.

The commonplace saying that tastes are not debatable is only partially true. *It is truer to say taste is a matter of beauty than to say beauty is a matter of taste.* The diversity of beauty is so much the refracted light of the glory of the Holy One that doing the beautiful — aesthetics (whether intentional or not) — is a constitutive part of doing the good — ethics (whether intentional or not). This does not mean that ethics is subsumed under a general rubric of aesthetics. But it does mean at least two things: that ultimately the good and the beautiful are properly defined and lived together; and that the identifying obedience of the people of God is a matter of actively taking delight in the Word of God by whom all things were made, in whom all things cohere, and in whom all shall finally be gloriously recapitulated. The sovereignty, majesty, power, and glory of God are descriptions of efficacious beauty. Free, spontaneous obedience is the creature's active delight in the law of the One who is the source and the criterion of purifying love.

The Holy and Conversion of Delight

Tempting though it might be, we are not now going to embark on a general aesthetics in the form of an analysis of the phenomenon of delight from which then to get a glimpse of what God's delight might be and its relation to holiness. Rather, we shall try again to ask about cruciform knowledge and, in this case, see some of the scandalous things a theology of the cross might mean for the relation of holiness and beauty.[1]

1. The most thorough and nuanced discussion of the inherent connection between beauty and the glory of God remains that of Hans Urs von Balthasar, for whom clearly aesthetics are not incidental to theology proper but at its very core. See

We should make no mistake: putting crucifixion and beauty in the same sentence is itself a frightful scandal. Where else than in this way of the cross is cosmic ugliness more blatantly shoved in our faces? And where else is the ready recourse to romanticism about the beauty of heroic self-sacrifice more intolerable? Maybe here, exactly on this point, we have the ultimate reason for apophatic theology, a reason that goes far beyond the intellectual problem of putting finite and infinite categories together.

But exactly on this point, Dürer's *Ecce Homo* has it right. The pain, mockery, blasphemous ugliness is not the end: the vindicated and the accursed one are the same. The relation between the cross and the resurrection is only partly one of before and after. The relation between cross and resurrection is also — perhaps primarily — one of lesser truth to fuller, one of reality to greater reality, one of more hidden to more manifest. Neither exaltation nor humiliation exists without the other — but they are not ultimately equal.

The weight of worldly evidence and wisdom to the contrary, the end of the cross is not death, defeat, suffering, abandonment, but life, victory, joy, reconciliation — *a contention which rings true when made not as a cloying consolation but as a retrospective confession of a struggling faith.* If what we mean by beauty has centrally to do with honesty, authenticity, truth telling, then the congruent simplicity of the artist's action will heighten, not suppress, the tensioned reality of life in this world.[2] Is this beauty — this congruent expression of tensioned reality — ever encountered unalloyed with its fraudulent substitute in this world? Obviously not; and the lust for such hypothetical unalloyed beauty is behind the illusion of beauty devoid of love and power and justice. In fact, what we mean by the beautiful is the expression of love, power, and justice

---

also Barth's treatment of beauty as one of the indices of theology done freely, joyfully; and, in this connection, see his informed appreciation of Mozart. That doxology as characteristic of all vital theology — a truism for most of Eastern Orthodoxy — is given new attention in, among other works, Geoffrey Wainwright's volume simply entitled *Doxology* (New York: Oxford University Press, 1980).

2. See Esther de Waal, *Living with Contradictions* (San Francisco: Harper and Row, 1989).

rightly related to evoke the delight of truthful recognition — whether that recognition be mainly of one pole of the tension or the other pole.

Whatever its sources, there is a widespread sentiment that holiness is not delightful. The supposition is that delight and sanctity are only theoretically compatible, and in fact the cultivation of one entails the suppression of the other.

This sentiment is not entirely alien to a part of the Reformed tradition — the part with a mortal fear of confusing the creature with the Creator, and with a correlative fear that the attraction to worldly beauty will interfere with the joy to be sought only in the Highest Good who is God. However, as with so many beliefs and practices of such a broad stream as the Reformed tradition, this atrophying suspicion of aesthetics is only part of the story. In fact, a rich theology of the beautiful is integral to a Reformed understanding of holiness. *It is not just that holiness is beautiful; it is that beauty in its awesome diversity is penultimately hallowed, and that holiness and beauty are in actual practice mutually defining. The surprise of the newly beautiful is integral to human wholeness, just as the prophetic critique is integral to distinguish between beauty and sentimentalized deceit.*

God delights in holiness. It is God's delight in something that makes it beautiful. *Beauty is in the eye of the Creator before it is in the eye of the creature.* A thing's or action's or person's beauty is grounded in this divine acceptance — a parallel in aesthetics to the imputation in which new creation is grounded in justification. Its inherent beauty consists in the fact that it is well pleasing to God. It is in God's seeing it that it is good. Holiness is not an addition to beauty. Holiness is God's operative delight in and for another which constitutes the beauty of the other.

We say we are "struck by the beauty" of this or that. We say someone or something is "striking" or of "amazing beauty." Without being aware of the awe alluded to in such words, we say this or that is "wonderful" or "astounding." Such speech is a remnant of the ancient wisdom that there is a numinous quality to beauty. This ancient wisdom seems to be acknowledged when we say someone is awakened by the "tremendous" effect this or that beauty has had. *Prior perspectives are displaced by new ones to such an extent that we cannot recall how we could possibly have seen things as we used to.*

Astonishment is one of the most reported effects that the presence of the kingdom has upon people. The coming of Christ is expected, but people are amazed at the signs of the end times when they actually are done and at the manner of their doing by Jesus. It is almost the case that the clearer Jesus' teachings and the more manifest his deeds, the more amazing and scandalous the response. I think of his reading from the prophet Isaiah in the town in which he was raised, and the reaction to his claim that "This day is this fulfilled in your sight." I think also of what he does — the activity which redefines rest — on the Sabbath to keep it holy. The *shalom* he brings redefines peace, and those who follow him find themselves caught in the paradox of letting go their life only to find it.

The presence of the kingdom exposes, searches, reverses according to the vision sung by the blessed Theotokos. The vision of the Day of the Lord sung in the *Magnificat* is about the radical reversal in store for everyone in the end times, and the call of this reality is for repentance. Here in the *Magnificat* justice and doxology are the content one of the other: what is pleasing to God is celebrated in song and deed. It may be an obvious point, but if so it is often assumed or undervalued; namely, that this praise is one of taking delight in what God wills: "Let it be to me according to your Word" means that Mary delights to do the promised purpose of God, and to do so in the face of the greatest risk and improbability imaginable. Mary's freedom for the Word is the opposite of grudging, resentful, calculating obedience. It is the kind of delight which redefines delight, just as the peace of the kingdom redefines peace. Freedom for the Word does not mean the loss of delight but its recovery and then some: for the recovered delight is good pleasure at a reality that one could not even possibly have dreamed of in advance, and at a cost not imagined in advance.

Besides the song of Mary, there is another incident which exposes the intimate relation between the recognition of the presence of the kingdom of God and beauty: the anointing of Christ with the precious oil. The more useful thing, as Judas was correct in pointing out, would have been to sell the ointment and give the proceeds to the poor. After all, had not Jesus all along made the poor a special focus of much of his teaching and preaching? Yet here we have this prodigal woman who anoints the Anointed One. In this costly proclamation she may intend to ratify Christ's identity; she may even intend to anticipate what is done to prepare bodies for burial. The important thing, however, is that as far as we can tell from the story, we do not know what she intended; what we do know is that Christ received the outpouring of the oil and said of it simply that she had done a beautiful thing. Here we have Christ, in his praise of her, placing beauty as the most appropriate response to his presence. Her action is well pleasing in his sight, and she will be remembered for the beautiful thing she did. In her own way this woman is also blessed among women.

Such holy delight presupposes a purpose, will, aim of God for his people. This supposition is described in many ways in the different forms and times of biblical literature, and no single description of it can afford to crowd out the others. Having said that, however, we cannot afford to miss one of the chief ways that will or purpose is described, namely, as *that which is pleasing to God.* Some of the roughest anthropomorphisms get expressed in these terms, not the least of which is the wrenching caprice which seems to be at work in God's favoring the one brother's sacrifice and not the other's. But it also takes on a deeper and more demanding ethics when the displeasure of God is invoked against the injustice done to people, and when God's love for the people is likened to the love a faithful spouse has for an unfaithful spouse. God takes delight in that kind of worship in which just deeds and sacrifices are joined, and the false worship divorced from justice is repugnant to him.

Whatever else Christ's baptism means, the words heard — "This is my beloved Son in whom I am well pleased" — are essential to understanding the full impact of that narrative. Of course there is the parallel with the testing of Israel in the desert before entering the Promised Land; of course there is the retroactive confession of the Evangelist that at this moment the Messiah's identity was made manifest — hence the practice of the season of Epiphany having more to do with Jesus' baptism than with the three sages following a star. Even then, the patent point about the star is not Chaldean astronomy but the universality of the light which lightens the Gentiles, for which punch line Luke waits until the presentation of Christ in the temple and the Messiah's reception by Simeon and Anna, kept alive, expectant, for this fit pregnant time, this *kairos* of the Lord's doing. Yes, of course, Christ's baptism means this and more — like his establishing solidarity with sinners needing baptism, baptism as part of the incarnational momentum of the eternal Word.

But whatever else is meant by Christ's baptism, this cannot be missed: "This is my beloved Son in whom I am well pleased." In Mark and Luke these words are addressed to Jesus, which may be the point of the declarative-accomplishing character of God's address. More likely, however, is the making public of that which, again according to Luke, was apparent to faithful Israel kept expectant for the events recounted in Luke 1 and 2. That making public is a confirmation again of this Messiah's identity as fulfillment of Isaiah's proclamation of what manner of Anointed One is God's. Isaiah 42:1 has it:

> Behold my servant, whom I uphold,
> my chosen, in whom my soul delights;
> I have put my Spirit upon him,
> he will bring forth justice to the nations. (RSV)[3]

That in which God delights is above all justice. It is God's delight that in the precedent sense is holy. Human delight is holy insofar as it is derivative of the delight of the Holy One. Now, the derivative holy de-

---

3. Note the Vulgate *"complacui"* of Luke 3:22 and what belongs with it: "Et ipse Iesus erat incipiens quasi annorum trigenta, ut putabatur, filius Ioseph, qui fuit Heli, qui fuit Mathat. . . ." In Luke the saying is not "this is" but "you are": *"su ei ho huios mou ho agapētos, en soi eudokēsa (in te complacui mihi)."* Note also the translation Jerome gives "loving one another," *diligatis,* which makes the connotation: this is my commandment, that you delight in one another, you pass on to each other and you receive from one another, the delight after the manner of my relation of my Father to me and of me to the Father (John 14–16).

light of God's people is to hear and do the Word — and that is exactly what makes the difference between practicing the law as an act of Christian freedom and killing oneself and others by trying to do the law out of servile fear. In the Reformed tradition at least, that is why so much attention is given to the third use of the law — as we have already noted. But here we need to note that being covered by the garment of Christ's righteous, practicing, free obedience to the law is the same as having a good, or free, conscience. And this has enormous consequences for understanding the dynamics of doing and recognizing the beautiful as a form of holiness, especially with the way the conscience which remains in all people is compared with the conscience those have who know God to be benevolent. Even in those who are most hardened, coarsened by sin, there remains a reminder of the image of God in which they were created.[4]

Though not the basis for a saving knowledge of God without the service of Scripture, a "sense of the divine *(sensus divinitatis)*" — Calvin's own words — still exists in every person. We, however, need to push this insight further. According to Calvin, the image of God in which humans are created is known most fully from its restoration. *Since it is the image of God in which all men and women are created, what is known to be in all men and women is not just a sense of the divine but a sense of the human.* What is restored in Christ is humanity created in God's image — and that means that the *sensus divinitatis* includes a *sensus humanitatis*. This sense of the human may be as obscured and distorted as the sense of the divine gets with the egocentric predicament. But it remains as a reminder, as a hunger for some unnamed nourishment, as a restlessness for our truer selves, and as a rebellion against settling for less than dignity and belonging and counting for something. This is where Augustine is perennially pertinent: "Thou hast made us for thyself, and our hearts are restless until they rest in thee" (opening of the *Confessions*). We need

---

4. On Irenaeus's (especially in *Adversus Haereses* 4.38.1) treatment of Adam and Eve's being created as child in the image of God, and the consequences of this view for Irenaeus's doctrine of soteriology as recapitulation, see Jean Daniélou, *Gospel Message and Hellenistic Culture,* vol. 2 (Philadelphia: Westminster, 1972), pp. 398-408.

to recognize the aesthetic implications of this claim: the *sense of the human* functions as an aesthetic faculty in every person.

I am not making the claim that this understanding of an aesthetic faculty accounts for all aesthetics, nor — surely — that one need accept this understanding to recognize and nourish beauty as diversely defined and experienced. But I am calling attention to a dimension of an understanding of beauty which is inherent in the Reformed tradition's anthropology; and I am calling attention to the basis for affirming an aesthetic faculty which is realistic about the role which recognition of the unbeautiful, the distorted, and the fraudulent plays in the prophetic discernment essential to the congruence of beauty and holiness. The shock of the incredibly ugly — I think here of the attention Bonhoeffer gives, in his *Ethics,* to shame and the capacity to be shocked — is a correlate of recognizing the good and the beautiful. That is why so often "nice" art is so much more distasteful and tedious than an unflinchingly honest expression of the ugly realities an artist also perceives.[5]

We have noted that revelation is a matter of being encountered by the One who is at once God Revealed and God Hidden — not two gods but the One who is hidden in his revealedness and revealed in his hiddenness. This carries over into the aesthetic act, whereby beauty encounters us simultaneously hiddenly and openly. *An abstract, an ideal, is simply inaccessible: rather, the only access we have to complex beauty is through congruent simplicity.* I have the impression that some aspects of Zen aesthetics are saying much the same thing. Whether or not that be true, at least this aesthetic realism is what is meant by integrity of recognition and expression, a way of defining the beautiful on which Calvin drew heavily.

Macrocosmic and Microcosmic Beauty

For Calvin *integrity* is where holiness, beauty, and doxology are mutually defined. There is a concise summary of this point when Calvin says, "He [God] everywhere commends integrity as the chief part of wor-

---

5. Cf. Iris Murdoch's novel *The Nice and the Good.*

shiping him. . . . By this word he means a sincere simplicity of mind, free from guile and feigning, the opposite of a double heart" (*Institutes* 3.6.5).[6] Integrity, as Calvin uses it, is characteristic of piety in all its expressions — in all that makes up one's daily life, that which is explicitly the service of God in cultic action, and that which belongs to a person's whole disposition, propensity, affective knowing and doing. *Integrity is congruence between a person's or thing's phenomena and the end for which that person or thing was created.*

Integrity is as much a basis for defining the beautiful as it is for defining the good and the holy. It is an aesthetics which draws on biblical observation and interpretation. It is an aesthetics, though, which is also deeply indebted to those classical authors who defined the good and the beautiful in terms of what is congruent with the purpose for which something or someone is created.[7] The *aesthetics of congruent simplicity* is at work when we, often unconsciously, judge something to be fitting, seemly, appropriate, apt, proportional, attuned, consonant, and so forth.

For this tradition of aesthetics, ornamentation and superfluity obscure the congruence between a thing and its true end. That which delights, attracts, turns the heart in wonder is where the underlying reality

---

6. This definition comes in that section of the *Institutes* which sometimes circulated separately and, among other Christian humanists and among evangelical Roman Catholics, pseudonymously as a treatise on the Christian life. Calvin brought it forward from the 1539 edition into the final edition of the *Institutes*. As is the case with most of the 1539 material, the section on the Christian life has a breadth and equanimity which predate some of the bitterest disputes into which Calvin was drawn.

7. Hence the attention given to discerning the end for which this or that is, as with the opening question of the *Shorter Westminster Catechism* and with Jonathan Edwards's treatise on the chief ends for which God created the universe. The nature of a thing or person is that into which one is created to grow; the good and beautiful are not so much the finished product as the right growth, i.e., the growth into that for which it was created. We have already encountered this idea in Irenaeus's description of the wholeness into which Adam and Eve were created. Cf. also H. R. Niebuhr's *The Responsible Self* (New York: Harper and Row, 1963), dealing with the third form of asking the ethical question and with the responsible person as *homo interpretans* (whose question is not what is legal or feasible but what is fitting).

breaks through by honesty, plainness, transparency, clarity, "sincere simplicity." Clarity as unclouded, unobscured is quite the opposite of flattery, niceness, guile, deceit. The honest depiction of an unjust and aesthetically repugnant condition is fit as a *via negativa* by which the real is disclosed.[8]

Reality and interpretation are inseparable in the aesthetic act, be that of the artist who sets the interpretive creativity in motion (say, the painter who applies color to canvas) or the artist who re-creatively interacts with the painting confronting him or her (say, the observer struck by the painting). But reality and interpretation are not the same nor of equal weight in the aesthetic act. Both the painter and the observer struck by the painting are responding to a prior reality which draws them out, astonishes them, quickens them, evokes in them a shock of recognition, radically alters a prior way of viewing reality.[9]

We have been mentioning figures who belong to the same broad aesthetical tradition as Calvin, before and after him. Now we need to note a rather specific feature of how integrity works, according to Calvin, in the dynamics of delight. He was fully aware that in his treatment of delight he was following Augustine's lead: grace brought about the conversion of delight by which a person moved from taking highest delight in self to the restoration of highest delight in God, which ordering then restored subordinate delights to their full strengths.[10]

---

8. Keats is later speaking from this aesthetical tradition when he repeats the observation that "Truth is beauty and beauty is truth. That is all you know and all you need to know." Only when understood as part of this larger aesthetic tradition does this otherwise overly naive and cryptic saying make sense.

9. I think of van Gogh's paintings of the potato eaters which could not be sold because to the market they did not look like real people, whereas in fact the reality of their lives was never more honestly disclosed. I think also of the furor created by Picasso's *Ladies of Avignon,* supposedly shocking because the rules of perspective were violated but really shocking because the painting effected a surcharge of new perspective. Through the painting there happened a recognition or acknowledgment of being confronted by reality at a far deeper level than ever before.

10. For the use Augustine's psychology makes of delight and yearning, see Peter Brown, *Augustine of Hippo* (Berkeley: University of California Press, 1969), pp. 154-57.

Calvin was also aware that in comparing the microcosm to the macrocosm he was following the lead of a wide range of ancient (and Renaissance) authors, and not just those in the Pythagorean and Platonic traditions. In his use of this comparison, Calvin makes the connection between delight, integrity, and beauty. Sane delight comes from being confronted by the beauty of the macrocosmic reality. The macrocosm holds before us a realm of things, movements and order, which are supremely congruent: there is an inner coherence between their appearance and the end for which they are created.

This sane delight comes about in us human observers, however, because there is a corresponding, though partial and broken, micro-universe. "Like recognizes like." This is different from saying that "same recognizes same." The microcosm is not the macrocosm, as decay and corruption make so inescapably clear. Like recognizes like. This recognition is the delight in integrity. *Sane delight belongs to integrity because delight is part of the end for which humans are created* — at least according to Calvin.

Calvin uses two loaded words for how we are to consider the macrocosm: "contemplation" and "meditation."

If we chose to explain in a fitting manner how God's inestimable wisdom, power, justice and goodness shine forth in the fashioning of the universe, no splendor, no ornament of speech, would be equal to an act of such magnitude. There is no doubt that the Lord would have us uninterruptedly occupied in this holy meditation; that, while we contemplate in all creatures, as in mirrors, those immense riches of his wisdom, justice, goodness, and power, we should not merely run over them cursorily, and, so to speak, with a fleeting glance; but should ponder them at length, turn them over in our minds seriously and faithfully, and recollect them repeatedly. But because our purpose here is to teach, it is proper for us to omit those matters which require long harangue. Therefore, to be brief, let all readers know that they have with true faith apprehended what it is for God to be Creator of heaven and earth, if they first of all follow the universal rule, not to pass over in ungrateful thoughtlessness or forgetfulness those conspicuous powers which God shows forth in his creatures, and then learn so to apply it to themselves that their very hearts are touched. The first part of the rule is exemplified when we reflect upon the greatness of the Artificer who stationed, arranged, and fitted together the starry host of heaven in such wonderful order that nothing more beautiful in appearance can be imagined; who granted to others a freer course, but so as not to wander outside their appointed course; who so adjusted the motion of all that days and nights, months, years, and seasons of the year are measured off; who so proportioned the equality of days, which we daily observe, that no confusion occurs. It is so too when we observe his power in sustaining so great a mass, in governing the swiftly revolving heavenly system, and the like. For these few examples make sufficiently clear what it is to recognize God's powers in the creation of the universe. Otherwise, as I have said, if I decide to set forth the whole matter in my discourse, there will be no end. For there are as many miracles of divine power, as many tokens of goodness, and as many proofs of wisdom, as there are kinds of things in the universe, indeed, as there are things either great or small.[11]

Delight and enjoyment are, for Calvin, characteristics of true knowledge of God and of self. In one of the most important condensations of his thought on the nature of this knowledge, Calvin says, "Here again we ought to observe that we are called to a knowledge of God: not that knowledge which, content with empty speculation, merely flits in the brain, but that which will be sound and fruitful if we duly perceive it, and if it takes root in the heart. For the Lord manifests himself by his powers, the force of which we feel within ourselves and the benefits of which we enjoy" (*Institutes* 1.5.9; pp. 61-62).

11. Calvin, *Institutes* 1.14.21; pp. 180-81 in the edition edited by J. T. McNeill, translated by F. L. Battles, 2 vols. (Philadelphia: Westminster, 1960). The parenthetical references in the text are to the location in the *Institutes,* followed by page references in the McNeill edition.

This right knowledge of God does not come partly from Scripture and partly from nature, which, as it were, would supply what is wanting in the knowledge of God we have from Scripture. Rather, contemplation of the microcosm and contemplation of the macrocosm are mutually reinforcing since the contemplation of either directs us to the contemplation of the other. That is because — as the passage above, about the affective characteristic of true knowledge, tells us — what we know from the microcosm and the macrocosm is not just that they are manifestations of God's power and wisdom but that they also disclose their chief purpose and value. Moreover, gloriously beautiful as the macrocosm is, unless we study the microcosm we shall not fully know this purposeful dimension, this value, of God's works.

> We must therefore admit in God's individual works — but especially in them as a whole — that God's powers are actually represented as in a painting. Thereby the whole of mankind is invited and attracted to recognition of him, and from this to true and complete happiness. Now those powers appear most clearly in his works. Yet we comprehend their chief purpose, their value, and the reason why we should ponder them, only when we descend into ourselves and contemplate by what means the Lord shows in us his life, wisdom, and power; and exercises in our behalf his righteousness, goodness, and mercy. (*Institutes* 1.5.10; p. 63)

One of the most disastrous effects of sin is that it nibbles away, erodes, corrupts, weakens the aesthetic action. The word "vitiate" is apt for this effect. The capacity to see the good and the beautiful, the appetite for the good and the beautiful, is not destroyed by sin, but it is weakened, debilitated, atrophied, misdirected by egocentric bondage. This means there is a strongly aesthetic dimension to conscience. Of course, there is a juridical tone to conscience. However, the dictates of the conscience are also assessments of the congruence or incongruence between a thing — thought or action — and the end for which it was created.[12]

12. That is why (and here I am going beyond Calvin to Jonathan Edwards's re-

The Aesthetic Function of the Word

On this decisive point there is quite a difference between Calvin and some of the narrower thinkers who name themselves after him. I refer to the role of Scripture in this delight of affective knowledge. Scripture is not necessary to aesthetics — and this means that they wrongly claim Calvin as mentor who suppose the quality of art is in direct ratio to an artist's Christian piety. There is such a thing as Christian art — but only if by that one means that what is portrayed is explicitly connected to narratives and symbols of the Christian religion, just as, say, Buddhist art or Marxist art does the same for those loyalties. But something is far more at stake in Reformed aesthetics than art as depiction of a tradition. What is at stake is the clarity, transparency, simplicity — again, in short, the integrity — with which prehensile reality — reality which grasps the artist and will not loosen its grip — is expressed in aesthetic passion.

Aesthetic integrity is practically the opposite of nice decoration, the opposite of so-called art functioning as propaganda, the opposite of glib oversimplification. Reality as we live it, as it comes to us, as it inescapably confronts all men and women, as we know it to be the human condition, is immensely complex. It is so laced with ambiguity and countervalences that aesthetic integrity means the ceaseless struggle honestly to point to and illumine that reality. *Reality as it grasps the artist is "tensioned." It presents itself, it has coherence, not with tension undone but with the dynamic tension disclosed: as with the simplicity of a vaulted ceiling. Aesthetic integrity is the practice of unflinching discernment and announcement of tensioned reality which is there prior to artistic discernment and announcement.*[13]

---

covery of Augustine's insight on this) Edwards had the experience, upon his conversion, of the restoration of delight to all his senses.

13. In commenting on the Lazarus story, Buechner observes the difference between sentimental prettiness and awesome beauty: "When they brought Jesus to the place where his dead friend lay, Jesus wept. It is very easy to sentimentalize the scene and very tempting, because to sentimentalize something is to look only at the emotion in it and at the emotion it stirs in us rather than at the reality of it, which we are always tempted not to look at because reality, truth, silence are all what we are not

That is why Calvin's imagery of the function of the Scriptures is so important, when he compares them to lenses through which we see the works of God more clearly than we could without them. The lenses are not there to help us see the lenses better. We do not use eyeglasses primarily to see glasses which help us see glasses which — and so on. The lenses enable us to see the wonder already there to be seen, studied, enjoyed, delighted in, overawed by. God's power is always manifest through his works, so that no one has a good excuse — as Paul in the first two chapters of the letter to the Romans argues — for not knowing God.

> [God's] presence [is] portrayed in his creatures. Despite this, it is needful that another and better help be added to direct us aright to the very Creator of the universe. It was not in vain, then, that he added the light of his Word by which to become known unto salvation. . . . Just as old or bleary-eyed men and those with weak vision, if you thrust before them a most beautiful volume, even if they recognize it to be some sort of writing, yet can scarcely construe two words, but with the aid of spectacles will begin to read distinctly; so Scripture, gathering up the otherwise confused knowledge of God in our minds, having dispersed our dullness, clearly shows us the true God. (*Institutes* 1.6.1; pp. 69, 70)

In this passage Calvin is talking about how saving knowledge of God comes about, and that is, for Calvin, different from the general knowledge which comes about through the personal and the heavenly universes apart from Scripture. That distinction is not to be blurred, for, according to Calvin, not all persons are moved to a saving knowledge of God. However, for the topic we are presently addressing — holi-

---

much good at and avoid when we can. To sentimentalize something is to savor rather than to suffer the sadness of it, is to sigh over the prettiness of it rather than to tremble at the beauty of it, which may make fearsome demands of us or pose fearsome threats" (Frederick Buechner, *Listening to Your Life* [San Francisco: Harper, 1992], p. 104).

ness and aesthetic action — Calvin's treatment of the function of Scripture provides a kind of model for the dynamics of aesthetic integrity.

There are at least two quite different ways of considering Scripture's function. One is to look to Scripture as a reservoir of infallibility. This way argues that Scripture's authority is its ability (with the work, of course, of the Holy Spirit in the composition and interpretation of the texts) to supply error-free truth. The other way is to look to Scripture as that which moves people to see themselves and others and the universe in a different light than they did before. This way argues that Scripture's authority is its ability (with, of course, the work of the Holy Spirit in the composition and interpretation of the texts) to supply an iconographic power for the transformation of the images by which people live and die.[14]

Surely these two ways of considering Scripture overlap in any single theologian; neither is totally without elements of the other. Nonetheless, one or the other is the operative and main understanding for any given person's theology. With which one Calvin mostly works is a matter of perennial debate and of tedious semantics. Here I am contending only two things. First, it is anachronistic to try to determine what position Calvin would take in some nineteenth-century preoccupations with literal infallibility, religious certainty, and scientific evidence. Second, and mainly, Calvin attributes to Scripture a power which goes far beyond legal or accounting or juridical categories, a power he often (not exclusively, but often) describes in aesthetic categories. On this ground Scripture functions as an instrument of disclosure, unveiling, clarity, exposure, honesty — in short, integrity, authenticity.

Moreover, one need not be a believer for Scripture to function this way. This contention is (to use one of Calvin's own figures) a slippery one with sides sloping to error if exaggerated in either direction. On the one hand, the Scriptures' primary function is within the community of belief to move men and women to a saving knowledge of God and self.

---

14. For a view similar to what I mean by iconographic power and knowing, see James Loder's treatment of imagination, in *The Transforming Moment* (San Francisco: Harper and Row, 1981), pp. 188ff. and passim.

On the other hand, the Scriptures also are uncannily apt for the un-flinching acknowledgment of the complexity, ambiguity, muddle of the human condition. The biblical realism is there whether or not the per-sons dealing with Scripture are themselves moved to accept and prac-tice the distinctive faith of the Christian community. That is why it is of immense importance that the book of Ecclesiastes is included in the canon: an unvarnished sense of futility also belongs to Scripture's hon-esty. *That honesty, and not some abstract supposed infallibility, makes Scripture not less but more God's Word. That honesty is a validation that it is not God's Word for some diaphanous creatures in a sentimentalized uto-pia but God's Word for struggling humans in this pied, brindled world.*

This point has been amply made by Auerbach and others, who note the striking candor of biblical narratives. It is also the point Flannery O'Connor tried again and again to make in the way she drew on Johannine paradoxes about blindness and seeing, in her novel *Wise Blood.* It is the point Chagall's paintings make over and over again, when biblical and nonbiblical images are brilliantly — illuminatingly — set forth, as mixed as the colors on a palette. It is the same point made, un-wittingly or not, in some circles of popular culture, in the lyrics of a singer like Mary Chapin Carpenter, of which her "Jubilee" is just one example. Then there are movies which struggle with the wrenching moral issues in which people are perennially entangled, be they on a monumental and unremittingly painful scale (for example, *The Killing Fields* or *Saving Private Ryan*) or on a smaller and inescapably ironic, though no less painful, scale (as with *Life Is Beautiful* or *Babette's Feast* or *Cinema Paradiso* or *Il Postino*). Other examples will jump to others' minds.

Beauty and the Sovereignty of God

We have invoked, above, the ancient distinction between microcosm and macrocosm. But there is another level which — though adding an-other neologism — I should like to designate the *mesocosm: the middle level between the including cosmos and the included cosmos.* Flannery

O'Connor speaks about "the middling planes of grace," and I think that may be what she also means. Mesocosmic beauty is what is identified and practiced in the commonweal among men and women. It is within the encompassing macrocosm and from the personal microcosm that justice is worked out, and it is part of the calling of the people of God to manifest in the political realm, as in a mesocosm, the beauty of justice. Here I must immediately add that the imagery for this mesocosmic beauty is almost as much that of a garden as of a city. In fact, planting and tending imagery and political imagery overlap and get mixed together, and they seem to need each other for correctives. Here, however, I am concentrating on seeing the polis as the mesocosmic sphere in which one is to exercise one's vocation. The calling is to approximate here and now, in this muddling world and in these *meantimes* — not in some Docetic utopia — the beauty of holy life together. To heed and obey this high calling is to be drawn forward by a vision of the accommodated glory of God in the form of a holy polis.

There have been two motivations in the way much of the Reformed tradition has consciously dealt with the beauty of human invention: *iconoclastic rejection* and *edifying simplicity.* Both are positive in their aim at simplicity, spareness, minimalism. They both aim at simplicity congruent with the essentially simple glory of God which we experience as purifying love. And both are positive in their aim to identify and worship the true God whose being toward his creation is celebrated in the aesthetic — and in the political — act. That is, both see the vital connection between the sovereignty of the living God and the specific simplicity which is congruence with this particular God's glory. In political terms these two impulses are the overthrow of tyrants, on the one hand, and the upbuilding of the commonweal according to rightful rule, on the other.

In this practice of congruent simplicity, however, the one impulse cuts away — prunes — whereas the other impulse nurtures — grafts. The one primarily begins and ends with the prohibitions of the second commandment. The other begins with the second commandment and continues with the imperative to gather and to plant and to build up. *The pruning or iconoclastic impulse and the grafting or iconographic impulse so belong together that each needs the corrective, complementary pressure of the other. Reformed aesthetics and Reformed political theology have been the history of the interplay of these two efforts at congruent simplicity.*[15]

The danger of holiness is a gracious fact. It is not a matter of having the danger weighed over against the safety. Encountering, being encountered by, the Holy One inescapably brings with it, has as part of its content, uprooting, purifying, pruning, overturning the false securities of cheap grace in whatever form. So before we go further in speaking about the beauty of holiness, we need to reiterate: the glory of God of which we speak is that known and efficacious above all in the cross of the promised Messiah who is Jesus who taught and demonstrated the presence of God's new order. This is the same Jesus Christ who was obedient unto the death on that cross, who was raised from the dead, who anointed the many with the power of the Holy Spirit, who is the Lord and who "will come again in great glory to judge the living and the dead, whose rule will have no end."

So, is this destiny beautiful and glorious? If so, then every natural fiber in us quite accurately responds not with ordinary delight, but with fear and dread unto death. There is a profound difference between awe before God's glory — the fear of the Lord which is reputed to be the beginning of wisdom — and an institutionally perpetuated fascination with death. That fascination can take the form of progressive withdrawal from others and the world or of progressive aggrandizement of self at the expense of others and the world. There are a dread and fear unto life, dread and fear which are components of repentance, of contrition, of daily mortification. Repentance is all the more accurate and deep exactly because it belongs to the discovery that the encountering Holy One is that love who will not let us finally fall outside ultimate be-

15. These two senses, which I call the pruning and the planting sides of the same quest for simplicity, are parallel, I think, to the distinctions Peter Maastricht makes in his discussion of the holiness of God (cited in Karl Barth, *Church Dogmatics* II/1 [Edinburgh: T. & T. Clark, 1957], p. 539: from Mastricht, *Theoretico-practico Theologia* [1698], 2.19.5f.), "segregation," "dedication," "representation," and "detestation." The first and the fourth roughly correspond to what I see as the pruning or iconoclastic impulse, the second and third to the nurturing or repleting impulse.

nevolence. That love cannot forever be successfully resisted. The Holy One will see to the fulfillment of *shalom* for all creatures, including sinners who have been forgiven into being a new creation.

When we have more or less got it straight that what is meant by holy delight is costly life, then we can see something of the way understanding holiness as purifying love helps us understand better what is meant by the glory of God and the commonweal of God. Holy delight is a response to God's glory as accommodated benevolence. We now can attend to two implications of this recovery of the essential loving nature of God's glory.

The first implication is that the manifestation of God's glory is one of sheer compassion. This is quite a different emphasis than is often called to mind when one speaks of the glory of God. *The glory of God has become unfortunately closely associated with the* mysterium tremendum *divorced from the far greater reality of which fear is only a part, namely, the* mysterium adorandum. Again, I am somewhat apologetic for adding another term to our discussion: *mysterium adorandum;* but so often the mystery to be feared is spoken of without the specification of the adoration which the mystery of God's glory evokes — that God whose very being is love. Indeed, the love evoked by purifying love includes awe and wonderment. It sends Jacob limping forward with the new identity as Israel. It sends Moses (with Aaron's company — not a minor point) stammering back into Egypt to deprive Pharaoh of his slave labor. But the point is that all this activity of God's love toward the creature is a strategy, an economy, of God's benevolence.

That God's is a strategy, an economy, of love remains hidden in its appearance and apparent in its hiddenness. Just ask the Egyptian horses and their riders over whom the sea closed; and just ask Saul, who forfeited his kingship because he disobeyed God's orders to take no prisoners; and just ask Job, who on top of everything else had to endure the advice of his friends; and above all just ask the Holy One of God, who is not faking when he prays that if it be the Father's will the cup pass from him. *Vindication of God's benevolence is almost always retrospective.* That at least is the point of chapters 11 and 12 of Hebrews: the end, the purpose, of the endurance suffered by those who went before was not seen by them. They shared proleptically, anticipatorily, in the experience of those living in the last times. This retrospectivity of our confession of God's providence is part of the secret discipline of Israel's and the church's cultic memory. Though we deal with this more amply in the next chapter, here it is helpful to see that the cultic memory of God's people includes a highly selective reading and writing of past events. This cultic memory is proclamatory history whose aim is to shine back God's glory by "generating" — repeating it freshly so that each begetting, each generation, shares in it — hope in God in season and out of season.

As to the second implication, when we allow the beauty of holiness to control what we mean by God's sovereignty,[16] we get a significantly altered understanding of God's political purposes and human political responsibility. I take this struggle to get right the correlation between God's ruling and derivative human ruling to be not a weakness but a strength of the Reformed tradition. It is consonant with the seriousness with which the Old Testament is taken as canonical literature for the New Testament community then and now.

There is a middle term to glory and to rule: "majesty." The majesty of God is used synonymously sometimes with God's glory and sometimes with God's reigning power. One reason for this overlapping is the very good one that in its opulent imagery, the Bible frequently describes glory in political imagery and political power in terms of refulgent splendor. In doing this biblical writers and editors inevitably draw on successive cultural models, and thus do not differ from other Middle Eastern and Mediterranean seers. What is quite notable, however, is the content of the proclamation to which this common cultural heritage is turned. The startling thing is not that God is described in terms of glorious rule, but that a radical redefinition occurs in what is meant by glory

16. The habit of aligning God's sovereignty with God's transcendence or with his divine nature appeared when, as Moltmann observes in *The Crucified God* (New York: Harper and Row, 1974), p. 232, a certain strain of orthodoxy stated that despite the union of the two natures in Christ, God remains untouched in his sovereignty. Cf. W. Placher, "The Vulnerability of God," in *Toward the Future of Reformed Theology*, ed. D. Willis and M. Welker (Grand Rapids: Eerdmans, 1999), pp. 203-4.

and by rule. They indeed belong together: the rule and glory of the Holy One are reciprocally denoted. But what comes to dominate in Israel's expectations is the image of the shepherd King and the suffering servant Lord. Ultimately, self-giving for the sake of the people of the covenant is the hallmark of the Messiah, and compassion is the presupposition, the ground and the end, of ruling in glory.

That is why *the most radical thing is not the rejection of the language of kingship and queenship, but their being overturned to convey utterly new, scandalously quickening content.* The tyrants so define glory and rule that they take divine appointment to be a matter only between the divinity and themselves. Those who kill such usurpers tell themselves they are engaged in tyrannicide, never regicide. The distinction could well be all too neat and fine a point in practice; to the one being killed, and to his or her followers, such killing is regicide. It is not until, or unless, governance — by whatever political arrangement — is seen as a function of the covenant between God and the people and the ruler that tyranny of whatever order and at whatever level and in whichever corner is broken. God initiates the covenant with the people and with rulers whereby the people and the rulers alike have any rights at all. This three-way covenant is the foundation of a political responsibility to which both the designated rulers and those who share in their designation are called. This is the basis of a commonweal which, in this present age, affords the maximal possibilities of living humanely — or maybe just least destructively, which is already an improvement on many conditions. The worldly city, even at those moments when it is at its best, is not to be taken seriously as more than a remote approximation of the heavenly city. But a vision of the heavenly city has a drawing power — a shaping teleology, a reordering delightfulness — to it which already functions as prophetic and constructive critique of any and every worldly arrangement.

We have noted above Calvin's teaching in the *Institutes* that God's creative purpose is for delight, not just usefulness. This teaching is perhaps even stronger in his commentaries, sermons, and letters where, among other things, he gives a portrait of the righteous ruler. His sermons on 1 and 2 Samuel were preached very near the end of his life, at a time when it seemed that the king of France was the least likely candidate for the title Most Christian King. In these sermons Calvin notes one of the main points of these books. Despite Israel's insistence that it have a king like all the other nations, in his mercy God gives them a king who is completely unthinkable according to the kingly criteria with which the other nations work. That is brilliantly put in the scene where the prophet runs through all the presented and presentable sons of Jesse. When the prophet insists on asking whether there is anyone else, Jesse has to admit that, yes, technically, there is one more — but he is only a shepherd. As Calvin interprets it — and in this I think he is correct — it is just the qualities which make him a good shepherd that fit David to be anointed king. That is, in his benevolence God gives Israel a ruler who protects the flock, who leads the flock to nourishment — and who plays the harp and sings. Those who know something about herds and flocks know the comfort and assurance which the shepherd's voice and playing give those in his or her care.

It is not sovereignty which needs to be replaced if the prophetic word is to mean anything. What needs replacing is an oppressive or despotic or dictatorial or heteronomous perversion of sovereignty. What replaces the twisted sense is a sounder, more varied, richer, more biblically multiconnotational understanding. Paul Lehmann calls this dynamic the transfiguring power of the Word in, over against, and for the polis. God's benevolent, and eventually all-efficacious, care for the whole of creation includes that part of creation gone astray into bondage of sin. This all-inclusive, ultimately benevolent, and efficacious caring is, to put it idiomatically, a thing of great beauty.

This high calling is to the problematic exercise — as opposed to the less complicated abdication — of political power. Sins in civic matters are at least as much those of omission as of commission. The dictum that "power corrupts and absolute power corrupts absolutely" is, at best, only one side of the matter. Power to free, to right wrongs, to listen, to heal, to love, to accept love — all these forms of power run the risk of abuse; but these exercises of power need cultivation, not denigration. Moreover, it is frequently those classes with power who romanticize powerlessness. It is easy for the classes with power to warn the powerless about the corrupting dangers of power and so to hold it on behalf of the powerless! That is like the rich telling the poor about the dangers of becoming wealthy, hence their keeping the poor from the temptations of filthy money! The most serious vocation is the responsible use of power, which use may entail its strategic transfer to others but in any case its stewardship — instead of a simpler abdication out of a fear of failure, or guilt, or human disapproval. The ideal of accountable use of power is rather well formulated by Benet Syms:

> Servant leadership functions from trust in love as the corrective to fear — the fear that distorts leadership into struggles for subjugation and control. Repressive power in any system will always erupt in violence eventually. . . . In a world become too small for violence, power has no acceptable moral purpose except for empowerment to participate in power — in appreciative mutuality, freedom and dignity. Where freedom is the context of any form of human organization, members at all levels are harnessed to a loftier goal than competitive personal gain. The high purpose of servant-led systems — in families, schools, businesses and nations — is the inclusion of all its members in proportional responsibility for decision-making and the success of the system. Organizations so aimed will be enlargers of life for their people.[17]

In that difficult parable of the three men left with the talents until the master returns to demand an accounting, the one who comes in for the harshest judgment is the one who played it safe, took no risks, and buried the amount he was allotted. It is a difficult parable because, like most of the parables of the kingdom, it is repugnant to worldly wisdom. For example, the parable leaves unanswered the question of what would be the reward if the ones who did invest the amounts lost everything — which of course is the cautious servant's fatal fear. There are many layers of meaning to the parable, of course; but at least two things are clear. First, the presence of the kingdom introduces an urgency which makes

17. In *Turning Point* 17 (May-June 2000): 2; published by the Institute for Servant Leadership, Asheville, N.C.

calculation about ordinary rewards quite beside the point. And second, maybe the presence of the kingdom has the effect on people of changing the sets of things to which they spontaneously risk giving themselves. At least that would be consistent with Christ's praising the woman who rather than sell the oil for an obvious good work did, in this particular case, the even better work of beautifully prodigal outpouring. There is a sacramental quality to her act, and not to her act alone but to the acts of those caught up in the presence of the kingdom who struggle to live lives congruent with the end times. It is to the nature of this hope-filled living that we turn in the next chapter.

CHAPTER SIX

The Hope of Holiness

We have said something about one of the consequences of God's prior, singular holiness: namely, the radiation of God's glory to creatures who are thereby beautiful in the eye of their beholder. In this chapter we turn to another consequence of God's prior, singular holiness freely imputed to creatures, namely, that they are freed for the sure hope of growing in the perfect love in which they are already perfectly embraced.

Holiness and Perfection

Dichotomous questions abound when it comes to the relationship between perfection and holiness. Can anyone be really holy here and now, or is one's holiness reserved for heaven? Is not perfection a state of completeness, or is perfection an ascetic pilgrimage through a history of temptations? Are we actually righteous, or do we always remain forgiven sinners? And so on.

A clue to dealing with these forms of questions is the fifty-sixth question of the *Heidelberg Catechism:* "Q. 56. What do you believe concerning 'the forgiveness of sins'? A. That, for the sake of Christ's reconciling work, God will no longer remember my sins or the sinfulness with which I have to struggle all my life long; but that he graciously imparts to me the righteousness of Christ so that I may never come into condemnation."[1]

Growth in perfection would seem an absurdity. And of course, it is foolishness, the foolishness of the cross. According to God's wisdom, the disclosed mystery of God's purposes for all creation in Christ, there is an ultimate completion which is the scope, the end toward which we are drawn whose foretaste, anticipation, eager forwardness is that of being already here and now perfectly forgiven. This life of hope is a daily being transformed from one degree of glory to another, not escape from creatureliness and the grid of time, space, and energy. This meanwhile life of the perfectly forgiven is precisely living the gospel in the contingencies into which we have been thrown for a purpose even when, espe-

---

1. The *Heidelberg Catechism* presents the call to perfection as something which functions like the second use of the law, i.e., continually to move us to repentance and to spur our reliance on the Holy Spirit; it does not so much (as I intend here to do) see the call to perfection as indicative of the condition of those who practice their being perfectly forgiven (as a function of the third use of the law, which, after all, is what the *Heidelberg*'s main thrust is, given locating all of the third part of the catechism under the rubric of thanksgiving). Cf. D. Willis, "Forgiveness and Gratitude: The Doctrine of Justification in the Heidelberg Catechism," *Harvard Divinity Bulletin,* Oct. 1963, pp. 11-24. "Q. 114. But can those who are converted to God keep these commandments perfectly? A. No, for even the holiest of them make only a small beginning of obedience in this life. Nevertheless, they begin with serious purpose to conform not only to some, but to all the commandments of God. Q. 115. Why, then, does God have the ten commandments preached so strictly since no one can keep them in this life? A. First, that all our life long we may become increasingly aware of our sinfulness, and therefore more eagerly seek forgiveness of sins and righteousness in Christ. Second, that we may constantly and diligently pray to God for the grace of the Holy Spirit, so that more and more we may be renewed in the image of God, until we attain the goal of full perfection after this life" (Presbyterian Church, U.S.A., *The Constitution, Part I, Book of Confessions* [Louisville: Office of the General Assembly, 1994], p. 48). Growth in holiness — "more and more" — and the difference between perfection of a kind given us now in Christ and "full perfection after this life" are keys to this vision. I find the implications of this vision accessibly treated, with ordinary examples from lives filled with realistic ambiguities, in Lewis B. Smedes, *A Pretty Good Person* (San Francisco: Harper and Row, 1990). Mentioned above but always worth repetition is Esther de Waal's *Living with Contradictions* (San Francisco: Harper and Row, 1989).

cially when, that purpose is risibly hidden or apparently the opposite of benign.

The language used to discuss perfection is far from perfect, and in fact is something of a semantic morass which requires more draining of past assumptions about others' meanings before it can bear much fruit — and surely this is the case with the debates about what is globally called the Methodist doctrine of perfection. Here I can only indicate that an examination of John Wesley's most explicit sermon on the topic — and not on it as a topic but on Philippians 3:12-15: "Not as though I had already attained perfection, either were already perfect. . . . Let us, as many as be perfect, be thus minded" — makes clearer what Wesley did not mean by perfection than what he did mean. That sounds like a criticism of Wesley, but I mean by it a positive acknowledgment that perhaps the main reason for Wesley's doctrine on this point is that, clear or not, the Christian preacher is not free not to preach what is in Scripture: "We may not, therefore, lay these expressions aside, seeing they are the words of God and not of man. But we ought to explain the meaning of them; that those who are sincere of heart may not err to the right hand or the left, from the prize of their high calling."[2] In summarizing the sense in which Christians are not perfect, Wesley says,

> Christian perfection, therefore, does not imply (as some men seem to have imagined) an exemption either from ignorance, or mistake, or infirmities, or temptations. Indeed, it is only another term for holiness. They are two names for the same thing. Thus, every one that is holy is, in the Scripture sense, perfect. Yet we may, lastly, observe that neither in this respect is there any absolute perfection on earth. There is no *perfection of degrees,* as it is termed; none which does not admit of a continual increase. So that how much soever any man has attained, or in how high a degree soever he is perfect, he hath still need to "grow in grace," and daily to advance in the knowledge and love of God his Saviour.[3]

2. John Wesley, *Sermons on Several Occasions,* rev. ed. (London: Epworth Press, 1946), p. 457.

3. Wesley, pp. 461-62.

Philip Lee notes the shift from an understanding of the church as a mixed body to an inordinate preoccupation with a certain kind of purity of the church, the latter contributing to reinforcing a focus on the *self*.

> The change occurred because of the almost obsessive desire to establish a pure Church. Whereas Calvin had been convinced by the parable of the wheat and the tares as well as the history of the Church that God's Church on earth will always be an imperfect organization — an admixture of saints and sinners — later Puritans were determined that the Covenant people would be free of mixture and error. They interpreted the parable of the wheat and tares as an admonition to "gather the weeds first and bind them into bundles to be burned, but gather the wheat into my barn." It was from this pressing concern for the purity of the Church that the Great Awakening and the revivals which followed were to receive their impetus. Out of the revivals came the view that the subjective experience of God's salvation was a required mark of a Christian. Whereas classical Calvinism has held that the Christian's assurance of salvation is guaranteed only through Christ and his Church, with his means of grace, now assurance could be found only in personal experience of having been born again.[4]

I would only add that it was not just a preoccupation with the purity of the church — out of proportion to its unity, catholicity, and apostolicity — that led to this rather morbid fixation on the self's subjective experience of its own experience of salvation. The more fundamental detour was that while the quest for the purity of the church was correct, it defined that purity rather by the law than by the gospel. It bypassed the crucial definition of the church as that body of forgiven sinners who daily undergo mortification and vivification and who are dependent on belonging to Christ with the other forgiven sinners he has joined to himself. A prior definition of "purity" crept in which often as not (not

4. Philip J. Lee, *Against the Protestant Gnostics* (New York: Oxford University Press, 1987), p. 143.

exclusively) was at odds with the indicative that members of the body of Christ are precisely those who welcome others as Christ has welcomed them.

It is in a particular vineyard, season, soil, pruning, ripening, harvesting that we grow — not some other vineyard and so forth. Living the gospel is the grace-enabled coping with, working in and through the ordinariness of this finite and sin-prone and redemption-more-prone life. Discipleship is faithfully doing what comes to hand. However it may be with God's being in the details, discipleship is a matter of being faithful in the small things and with the other small people. Growth in holiness has to do with the extra mile walked, the next forgiveness practiced, the next cut bandaged, the next body interred, the next malicious rumor not shared, the next bill paid, the next coat given, the next letter written on behalf of, the next meal scraped together and served, the next chord struck and released, the next widow's mite offered, the next early morning feeding made and diaper changed, the next prodigal gesture of affection delighted in, the next hurt not repaid with hurt, the next feeble demonstration for a modicum of justice joined, the next batch of votes gotten out. Christian freedom is living the details here and now in the presence of eternity.

Here for our recall is a portion of Scripture, duplicable on this point with many other passages, which shows the interweaving of holiness, the saints' partnership in the gospel *(koinōnia . . . eis to euangelion),* prayer, and practical, consummating love. When perfection comes up in the Scriptures, it is in all its forms a variation on God's completing what he has beneficially, benevolently set out to do, has covenanted to perform. Paul, or whoever goes by that name in the Epistle to the Philippians, writes:

> I thank my God in all my remembrance of you, always in every prayer of mine for you all making my prayer with joy, thankful for your partnership in the gospel from the first day until now. And I am sure that he who began a good work in you will bring it to completion at the day of Jesus Christ. It is right for me to feel thus about you all, because I hold you in my heart, for you are all par-

takers with me of grace, both in my imprisonment and in the defense and confirmation of the gospel. For God is my witness, how I yearn for you all with the affection of Jesus Christ. And it is my prayer that your love may abound more and more, with knowledge and all discernment, so that you may approve what is excellent, and may be pure and blameless for the day of Christ, filled with the fruits of righteousness which come through Jesus Christ, to the glory and praise of God. I want you to know, brethren, that what has happened to me has really served to advance the gospel, so that it has become known in the whole praetorium and to all the rest that my imprisonment is for Christ; and most of the brethren have been made confident in the Lord because of my imprisonment, and are much more bold to speak the word of God without fear. (1:3-14 RSV)

One of the most important features of this passage is what it has to say about imprisonment. The main point is not that God is turning even this imprisonment to a purpose. The prior point is the fact that imprisonment and its ilk are facts of life also for those who believe the end times are at hand. The good news does not deliver believers from hardships of all kinds. In fact — so long as costly discipleship does not slip into another form of works righteousness — a special measure of endurance is in store for those who suffer the consequences, and enjoy the benefits, of struggling daily to be followers of Christ. Following along and consequences are inseparable: the title of Bonhoeffer's *Nachfolge* is more simply, more powerfully translated by "consequences" than by the more familiar "cost of discipleship." Christian hope, living in the last times, is realistic. Life together is realistic eschatology, and so it is a great deal more than realized eschatology.

The hope of the Christian community is realistic in the sense that it has to do with the real thing. You know: *res, realiter;* "really," "realism," "realistic." This contention about the meaning of realism is one I have intended repetitiously to make in each of the previous chapters. So again: hope is focused on the real thing; it has to do with the constitutive matter of faith, namely, the fidelity of the one on whom faith is focused.

Here all I want to make clear is that *hope which is realistic includes the experience of despair.*

I mean to say it that way because there are two sides of this point. First, just as true faith is never without the struggle with doubt, so vivifying hope is never without the struggle with despair. How could it be otherwise, if one is to live compassionately in this world with a compassion that extends even to oneself? Second, hope is more inclusive of despair than despair is of hope, for there is always the hope that out of experiences of despair a future can be envisioned after all. How could it be otherwise, if one is to realize that the dark night of the soul is integral to holiness?

The experience of despair would often seem to be as derivative from hope as the word is. At least it would seem that much of despair implies a hoped-for condition which stands in such stark contrast to one's perceived condition that the latter seems hopeless. The explosive reality of this contrast — desperation — is the material either for some newly envisioned alternative living or for acquiescence in dreamless sickness unto death. I am not sure the bromide "Hope springs eternal" is much comfort to those for whom life as they perceive it is mainly a series of shattered expectations, a series of unspeakable losses and suffering, made all the more unbearable by those who would prate about the meaning of it all. The cry of dereliction from the cross may be the only comfort, if any shredded comfort be left, for those who are born into pain and systemic cruelty, who cannot escape bone-grinding squalor, who die having glimpsed some possible way of surviving from day to day and have that also snatched from them.

I venture to say that those who place hope on one side and despair on the other understand neither. At least Christian hope includes the honest despair of those who can cry with Job's wife: "Curse God and die." Those words are as much the cry of the people of God as the almost insulting arguments proffered by those who came to call on Job and offer their viewpoints on the theodicy question. Job's wife's words come from one whose losses are beyond her bearing or anyone else's bearing. Whatever resolution (rather, tabling) of the issue which may be seen (perhaps only as an illusion) in the book of Job, the facts remain, first, that such dreadful losses do occur hour by hour somewhere to someone, and second, that nothing can ever "make up" for those losses. One would think that the evidences for despair would be so overwhelming that one should leave it there. And prophetic realism does indeed let that side of the matter stand, lest a zeal to tidy up contradictions distract from struggling to correct injustices.

And yet there is the incontrovertible fact of the stubbornness of hope, the remarkable forward proclivity, for which one ought to be prepared to give a defense. The resources for visioning an alternative life are many, perhaps as many, actually, as there are different persons in successively different conditions and moments. I wish here only to mention several of the most frequently offered interpretive views from which some people claim to draw a modicum of meaning for hoping. Before turning to the most scandalous one of these views, it will be profitable to acknowledge the attractiveness of a viable alternative.

The stoic vision needs to head the list of the alternatives to Christian hope. I say "stoic vision" to distinguish it from some of its crudely reduced stereotypes; and I am aware it is rather global to speak in the singular of the stoic vision, so let me take the rather practical version of it in Marcus Aurelius. This stoic vision is not to be confused with quiescent masochism, with submissive apathy, with bemused cynicism, or with blind obedience to one's perceived fate. Those surely are its dangers. However, it provided and provides great resources for ethical engagement, and the total rejection of it is as impoverishing as it is improbable.

There are three features which appear in some way in each of its forms. First, it argues that since happiness is negated by the thwarting of one's fondest expectations, the wisest course for the individual is the diminution of expectation. The discipline required for this is that of reducing one's emotions, of cultivating a feeling of detachment to persons or things of this world. This is an ideal not completely attainable, but it is nonetheless the way to free oneself for higher attainments — so long as one does not get too attached to those attainments. Second, underlying the appearance of free activity, even in the cultivation of apathy, is foresight, providence, not a personal providence which an individual supplies but one to which the individual submits if he or she is to cultivate apathy. Third, what we experience as novelty is in reality repetition of what has happened "before" (though there is some question as to whether one can on this scheme really speak of before and after) and what will happen again over and over in an endless cycle.

While there are legitimate objections to it, there are at least three practicalities of this stoic vision which we dare not miss.

First, it does not foster the least romanticism about suffering. Or rather — a point to which we shall return — suffering, the lot of so vast a number of persons, is seen to have no constructive value to it. Masochism and self-pity do not flourish in stoic soil. The same cannot be as confidently claimed for some perversions of the gospel.

Second, the stoic vision does not spend much energy on blaming. Who is at fault is moot. Bearing grudges is one of the emotions most to be shed in the quest for apathy. Or rather — another point to which we shall return — it sees little benefit in anger (and no need to distinguish between what our society tries nicely to sort out as the difference between appropriate and inappropriate anger) other than as an obstacle to be overcome in the practice of apathy. Inveterate complaining about obvious unfairness does not grow well in stoic soil. The same cannot be as confidently claimed for some perversions of the gospel.

Third, the stoic vision has room for irony. It presupposes enough cohesion of events (cyclical providence, in this case) to make the incongruence striking but not amazing. When we say that a person takes something philosophically, we — at least in contemporary English idiom — often use that word to mean stoically. We point to a wry sense of humor to describe a person who has seen enough suffering and foibles of the human condition to be nonbitterly unsurprised about almost anything — having "seen it all." Or rather — still another point to which we shall return — while it affords good protection against disappointment, it does not leave one utterly exposed to the fresh wonders of utterly new gifts. Rash enthusiasm and prodigal joy do not flourish in stoic soil. In cultivating controllable protection, some perversions of the gospel are as good as stoicism.

In sum, the stoic vision can serve well to combat paralyzing discouragement in the face of overwhelming odds. It may well be that the social-psychological origins of stoicism were closely related to the enormity of events which threatened to swallow up family, language, self. In any event, stoicism is the very opposite of quietism. It is the very opposite of inactivity legitimated by supposed utter disinterest — the opposite, in other words, of that which is popularly taken for apathy. One of the ironies is that stoicism fosters a certain detachment among individuals which frees them from the paralyzing fears about the consequences should they fail. Stoicism is commendably realistic in one sense. It avoids the draining and paralyzing effects of being incapable of modicum and interim compromises, of being perfectionist in demands made on self and others, of being so responsible for complete justice that one treats this motley, dappled world as no-place, utopia.

If it be not stoicism, then what outlook or vision can deal with the ethical problem of facing overwhelming odds, with the problem of that enormity which spawns despair? On this question, at the very least, the children of light must be as wise as the others. If Christian hope is not at least as wise as serpentine stoicism, then all so-called Christian gentleness is a far more serious form of escapism than stoicism ever was or is.

When we attempt a comparison between Christian hope and the stoic vision, it would be self-defeating to ask which one is more useful in dealing with the problem of despair engendered by the enormity — the apparently hopeless size — of the problems facing those with some sense of the disparity between what is and what promises to be. Paradoxically the utility, the practicality, of Christian hope comes only as a concomitant of going through the motions of one's identity. These irreducible motions of one's identity are effective signs which both indicate and further effect their referent. "Efficacious sign" is the venerable way of speaking about this phenomenon of identity-in-action. And that is what is at stake in the commandment to remember the Sabbath day to keep it holy.

Hope, at least in a Christian perspective, is the forward inclining of trust, the forward momentum of faith, born and nurtured, fed and disciplined, enjoyed and celebrated in the loving community which every day chooses life rather than death.

Pannenberg needs to be taken seriously when he comments on the uses and abuses of the terms "hope" and "future" and "eschatology," which cover too large an area to be specific without more careful definition. He is especially on guard against uses of "future" and "hope" which divorce the time of the kingdom from what he calls ordinary or real time (which may, so his critics say, beg the question), with the result that such overly disjunctive usages "mean that the eschatological future ceases to have any connection with real time, or does not differ from the present and the past." Roy Fairchild is getting, I think, at the same point when he wishes to make sure that hope has to do with the present recovery of imagining a future and with the present reinterpretations of one's past.[5] That, at any rate, is the reason I find it confusing to speak of the resurrection as a *creatio ex nihilo:* what is redeemed is not nothing, but precisely what needs redeeming and re-creating is the objective of the full redeeming person and work of Christ and is being proleptically realized in the body of Christ. There is such a thing as the radical discontinuity of the same person, which formulation holds together Paul's "I, yet not I but Christ in me." This manner of relating the continuity and discontinuity of the new being is also different from one which, in effect, would say, "Christ, yet not Christ but I in him." That formulation is blocked by the fact that it is the sinner who is forgiven and set in motion in a new life, who is converted.

Having supplied caution after caution against focusing on the human personality, Barth finally, in *Church Dogmatics* IV/2, paragraph 66 on "The Sanctification of Man" and subparagraph 4 on "The Awakening to Conversion," is able to make his strongest statement that there is a continuing creaturely "I" in the action of conversion. "How could it be sanctification of real man if man himself were not present in his inner and outer activity, if it took place at some supernatural height or depth without him? It certainly does not take place without him. It takes place to and in him. It involves the total and most intensive con-

---

5. Wolfhart Pannenberg, *The Idea of God and Human Freedom* (Philadelphia: Westminster, 1973), p. 199. Roy W. Fairchild, *Finding Hope Again* (San Francisco: Harper & Row, 1980).

scription and co-operation of all his inner and outer forces, of his whole heart and soul and mind, which in the biblical sense in which these terms are used includes his whole physical being."[6] From my reading of James Loder, the transforming moment means the dynamics of such an awakening and conversion which is an ongoing movement no matter how punctiliar its location may be in retrospection.

Hope, the opposite of wishful thinking, is being off-balance toward the Coming One. Hope is the forward falling, one stride at a time, of those who run the race that is set before them looking to Jesus the author and perfecter of our faith (Heb. 12:1-2). Those verses make sense only as an extension of chapter 11, whose summary is that "And all these, though well attested by their faith, did not receive what was promised, since God had foreseen something better for us, that apart from us they should not be made perfect" (11:39-40 RSV).

This completion takes place in a historical, communal continuum. To get it straight we have to speak of a vicarious perfection. This vicarious completeness is already and not-yet-fully realized in the testing, perseverance, and discipline of the community. Not in community in general but in that community which is united to Christ by the bond of the Holy Spirit, that community whose ultimate perfection is the completion of Christ's righteousness applied to us. It is through our comembership in the body of Christ that we anticipate, partially but really, the perfection to which we are drawn forward. And this life together is not just how we grow in perfection. Indeed, the quality, dynamics, compassion, testing, mutuality, complementarity of this life together in Christ are already here and now the content — no matter still partially actualized — of that holiness. This life together is an effective sign of perfection.

This is the prophetic realism of transformation, not just personally but certainly structurally, societally, economically, politically. Writing of the function of a paradigm of transformation, Russel Botman's words are relevant not just for South Africa.

---

6. Karl Barth, *Church Dogmatics* IV/2 (Edinburgh: T&T Clark, 1958), p. 556.

I have chosen to speak of "a theology of transformation" [rather than a "theology of reconstruction"] also because it suggests a paradigm of growth and formation rather than of engineering and mechanization. While it is necessary to think of reconstructing a new South Africa, it is important not to lose sight of the extent to which society is an organism that grows rather than a structure that can be dismantled and reassembled like a motorcar engine. It is a way of thinking about human beings that sets theology apart from any ideology of reconstruction. A theology of transformation calls for a change in the *forms* of acting and the *forms* of being (1 Corinthians 7:29-31). Therefore, it represents the calling of a society, a community, or an individual to reach beyond itself for its new form. . . . My proposal for a theology of transformation is not informed by the so-called new world order, or by a high regard for legality. It is informed by a Christology that takes the practices of Jesus seriously as a category that is formative to human identity. Conditions in South Africa call for a vocational paradigm that returns to the following of Jesus of Nazareth with the ultimate aim of continuing his liberative practices. Dietrich Bonhoeffer can point us in the right direction in the search for such a liberative Christology.[7]

It is crucial — so to speak — to recognize this life together as an effective sign, a miracle of the presence of God's new dominion. That is quite different from an apparently controllable cause, though making distinctions among various levels of causalities was a way of getting at the mediation of God's providential care. To put it in a nutshell, the vicarious life together in Christ means redoing, newly actualizing, the *implications* of Christ's once-for-all entering into the Holy of Holies; it does not — does not — mean redoing that *all-sufficient sacrifice* itself.

7. H. Russel Botman, "Theology after Apartheid: Paradigms and Progress in South African Public Theologies," in *Theology in the Service of the Church: Essays in Honor of Thomas W. Gillespie,* ed. W. Alston (Grand Rapids: Eerdmans, 2000), pp. 36-51, here pp. 47-48.

The vicariousness of life together does not, does not, mean that we work hard at emulating being the Messiah. The once-for-allness of the Messiah's redeeming person and work frees us for coping as gracefully as possible with the enormity — the critical mass, ambiguity, and recalcitrance — of the problems facing the world which God loves and which is the theater of Christian discipleship.

The reality of hope precedes and is the presupposition of the personal realization of hope. Oh, yes, of course, hope is also a personal emotional condition. But to consider hope in the first instance only as a condition of heart would be to repeat the error so often made this side of Descartes of considering faith and love as primarily, preeminently an emotional condition in which one finds oneself or which one has the responsibility to cultivate. Biblically, the preponderant treatment is the reverse: hope is a matter of being located within a forward-moving people, of being one to whom the covenanting promises, the steadfast Word of God, apply. The reality of the structures and dynamics of the community of hope based on the promises of the persevering God — those structures and dynamics mean that even when a person or a group of persons do not see in their lifetime the fulfillment of what they hoped for, they do not thereby cease to belong to the society of hope. In fact, even when in the depth of despair, a person does not fall outside the structures of the divine society of hope.

I am thinking here, of course, of Romans 8, where it is clear that we who do not know how to pray also do not fall outside the community of the Spirit who intercedes on our behalf. First and finally, Christ and the Holy Spirit intercede for us when we are in direst distress, despairing and sensing utter abandonment. For, according to this passage, our personally experienced meaninglessness is but a part of the way the whole of nature, the whole world, is going through the birth pangs of the last times. I am also, however, thinking of another implication of the passage mentioned above, the end of Hebrews 11 and the beginning of 12. Everyone mentioned in chapter 11 as examples of faith did not — did not — receive what was promised. A part of the scandal of the gospel is that what was promised them is received by their successors in the faith. That is the way of realistic hope. It seems clear to me that by far most people do not experience in their lifetimes the fulfillments which they hoped for. And it seems clear to me that there is very little correlation between living righteously and getting exemption from injustice in this life. Those who give assurances to the contrary, in the face of crippling despair and anger, are guilty of corrupt marketing practices. There is good reason that the book of Ecclesiastes, thank God, is in the canon.

Sabbath Rest and Unrest

In *Fiddler on the Roof,* when the eldest daughter's suitor is finally going to ask for her hand in marriage, the whole action is stopped by the beginning of the Sabbath, in that wonderful scene when the mother lights the candles and puts the covering over her head. And of course, that is the point: the action is not stopped but begins in joyful earnest. The marriage, this marriage between this woman and this man in this year and in this community, is uniquely what it is because of the identity of the community in which it occurs. The identity defines the action; and while action and identity are reciprocal, the particular act of marrying is a matter of living out a dynamic identity. A more efficient use of time, a more expeditious settling of wedding intent are put in their place — and they have a place — if they are truly the matters belonging to the identity of this community. In this sense utility follows identity. Usefulness indeed comes, but it comes only as a by-product of identity.

The point we have consistently noticed is here starkly in the open: the people's holiness (manifold holiness) is grounded in God's holiness (singular holiness), and God provides the media by which holiness proper (singular holiness) is accommodated historically to take as subordinate (manifold holiness) a reality which can truthfully be said of God's people. God is not presented as kidding when he says, according to Leviticus, "I the Lord your God am holy. . . . You shall be holy." The Levitical code is offered, commanded to that end: that Israel reflect and express the irreversibly prior identity of the Holy God, in belonging to whom Israel's identity consists. Remembering the Sabbath to keep it holy is one of the media of Israel's holy identity.

In the case of the Sabbath rest, the commandment is grounded not in Israel's need for cultic activity of some sort, but in what they took to be the priority of God's identity and activity. In the expanded version of the Decalogue, the reason for the commandment, and for all the commandments, is that God called Israel and spoke his identity — plus the special wherefore: "In six days the Lord made heaven and earth, the sea, and all that in them is, and rested the seventh day; wherefore the Lord blessed the Sabbath day, and hallowed it."

The same point is made by the structure of the Decalogue. Whether the commandments be counted as four and six or five and five, the holy remembrance of the Sabbath belongs to the table which has to do with loving the Lord your God with all your heart and mind and soul as the presupposition of rightly loving neighbor as oneself. The whole of the Decalogue, both tables, is the outworking of the prelude or preface: "God uttered these words and said, 'I am the Lord your God.'" Everything follows from that, and without that at the beginning, whatever follows is nothing.

Were Israel to be exhorted to do or not to do this or that as a general moral code, the self-inflicted expectation of holiness would issue forth either in death-dealing despair or in no-less-fatal illusions of inherent superiority. Nothing would have been learned from forty years of following the Presence in the wilderness, from the discipline of starting and stopping when the Presence advanced or stayed, the discipline of living day by day and night by night as God supplied the promised means of daily bread and water struck from rock. The ritual remembrance of the Sabbath serves not to perpetuate the rite but to reinforce the future in store as Israel brings to heart and mind in each new day the fidelity of the Holy One in the wilderness.

That is the clue to why the holy remembrance of the Sabbath takes the form it does, namely, that of the Sabbath rest. There is, today, a good deal of well-intentioned but wide-of-the-mark hype which would expand Sabbath "rest" into a "theology of leisure." The Sabbath rest serves the well-being of those who labor every other time, both to refresh wearied bodies and minds and so to quicken again the reason for that labor after all. The Sabbath rest stands as a bulwark against the alienation of one's labor from oneself, whether that alienation be one imposed by a corrupt economic system or by deceiving ourselves into thinking that rest is merely inactivity. Sabbath resting and holy activity are — at least for those who dare locate their identity in God's call — mutually defining, mutually corrective, and mutually strengthening.

It has been my experience that the last things Calvinists, secularized or not, need to dwell on are more arguments for losing themselves entirely in their work. Addiction to work can, and often is, an escape from the freedom to practice holiness. There is indeed such a thing as addiction to work. A busyness, a more-the-merrier compulsiveness, functions as ingeniously praise-gaining avoidance for many people. Whether or not there is an epidemic afoot in the opposite direction from a work ethic or not, I let pass here; there may well be a non–works righteousness, a status based on conspicuous leisure, which needs to be faced. It is sufficient here to suggest that in addition to just the need to attend to the proportion, the measuring out, of time to work and to rest, there is a need to distinguish more nuancedly among different qualities of both work and of rest, both of which are integral to Sabbath remembrance.

If we remember the root meaning of holiness as containing the element of set-apartness, we will see that the Sabbath rest means time which is set apart from other time. On separation from the world and being a sanctuary in it as the holiness of the people of God, Bonhoeffer is rather clear.

> Only God is holy. He is holy both in his perfect separation from the sinful world and in the establishment of his sanctuary in the midst of the world. This is the burden of the song Moses sang with the children of Israel after the perdition of the Egyptians, as he praised the Lord, who had redeemed his people out of bondage of the world. . . . Like God himself, the Holy One, the people of his sanctuary are also separated from all things profane and from sin. For God has made the people his covenant, choosing them for himself, making atonement for them and purifying them in his sanctuary. Now the sanctuary is the temple, and the temple is the Body of Christ. Hence the ultimate purpose of God,

which is to establish a holy community, is at last fulfilled in the Body of Christ. For that body has been separated from the world and from sin, and made the peculiar possession of God in his sanctuary in the world. God dwells in it with the Holy Spirit.[8]

There is an unmistakable change in what one does and in the intentionality of doing the different something. The most inclusive name for that different thing is rest. Not symbolic rest or spiritualized rest in the first place, but the change which restores the body and the spirit, which renews for the future, which makes for healing. Even though it may not be as widespread as Toynbee saw the pattern in history to be, unquestionably when it comes to holiness there is a timing and placing of withdrawal and return, of going out and coming back, of advancing and consolidating. Without the one, it is fatally easy to submerge oneself in much doing of exhausting religious activity and well-intentioned busyness. Without the other, it is fatally easy to submerge oneself in spiritualized coziness and ritualized elitism. But in their complementarity, in the way Israel moves and stays in response to the moving and staying of the pillar of smoke and fire, lies the itinerary of holy pilgrimage.

The Sabbath kind of rest brings with it and keeps alive a holy unrest.[9] Prophetic realism calls Israel to a special kind of remembrance —

8. Dietrich Bonhoeffer, *The Cost of Discipleship* (New York: Macmillan, 1965), pp. 305-7.

9. On the transforming restlessness of faith and hope, see Moltmann's description: "The risen Christ, and with him the resurrection hope, must be declared to be the enemy of death and of a world that puts up with death. Faith takes up this contradiction and thus becomes itself a contradiction to the world of death. That is why faith, wherever it develops into hope, causes not rest but unrest, not patience but impatience. It does not calm the unquiet heart, but is itself this unquiet heart in man. Those who hope in Christ can no longer put up with reality as it is, but begin to suffer under it, to contradict it. Peace with God means conflict with the world, for the goad of the promised future stabs inexorably into the flesh of every unfulfilled present. If we had before our eyes only what we see, then we should cheerfully or reluctantly reconcile ourselves with things as they happen to be. That we do not reconcile ourselves, that there is no pleasant harmony between us and reality, is due to our unquenchable hope. . . . This hope makes the church a constant disturbance in human

that which moves Israel to repentance and to renewing the covenant not just in cultic activity but especially in practiced righteousness. And that prophetic remembrance is upsetting, overturning, disturbing rest. Just think of the prophetic exposure of those — of us — who would substitute feast days and outward ritual for consequential ethics. That is why one must speak not just of Sabbath rest but of Sabbath unrest. There is no rest in the usual sense of the word, not doing much, when there is such systemic injustice, cruelty, disease.

There is another way of saying the same thing about the unrest which is also a function of Sabbath remembrance. It is to acknowledge what are for the Reformed the second and the third uses of the law. We have noted this already above, but it merits repetition. The first use is the civil, to facilitate the governance of a people or nation. The second is to drive us to Christ, to call us to repentance, to quicken the conscience — the condemning function of the law. This is a form of the good news, since it means that God has chosen not to leave us alone to the devices and desires of our own hearts. The third use is to guide, instruct, quicken those who are already freely justified by grace alone through faith. It is good news that we are held to the commandment to remember the Sabbath to keep it holy. This third use of the law corresponds, in Calvin's treatment of the matter, to the second part of Christian freedom. It is that those who are freed from works righteousness by having Christ's righteousness imputed to them are also guided in their Christian freedom by the law, including that of the commandment to Sabbath holiness.

The holy disturbance which is part of the Sabbath rest is, for the Christian community, put in the fullest perspective by Jesus' assurance that his coming brings peace — only in a radically redefined sense. And

---

society, seeking as the latter does to stabilize itself into a 'continuing city.' It makes the Church the source of continual new impulses towards the realization of righteousness, freedom and humanity here in the light of the promised future that is to come. This Church is committed to 'answer for the hope' that is in it (I Peter 3:15). It is called in question 'on account of the hope and resurrection of the dead' (Acts 23:6). Wherever that happens, Christianity embraces its true nature and becomes a witness of the future of Christ" (Jürgen Moltmann, *Theology of Hope* [New York: Harper and Row, 1967], pp. 21-22).

it is exactly on the point of what keeping the Sabbath means that Jesus encounters some of his most intransigent opposition. It is a scandal for him to make the point over and over again by his deeds, not just his words, that the Sabbath is made for humans — not the other way round. Those who are driven to Christ by the law are those who count the Sabbath to be the first day of the week, the day celebrating the resurrection of Jesus the Christ. Even more than before, the day of holy rest and unrest anticipates that peace which God wills for all creation, that toward which the whole of creation groans, that new creation whose presence is vindicated by the resurrection of the crucified one.

What the law promised for the keeping of the Sabbath is fulfilled with the resurrection. This radical shift is not abstract. It reshapes, turns around a community's cultic remembering. Those who observe the Sabbath interpret that observance more and more in the light of the event celebrated on the first day of the week. The first day quite literally stands as the first day of the new creation ushered in by the resurrection of the crucified one.

There are means of hope for appropriating the benefits of this fulfilling of the Sabbath promise in the day of resurrection. It is to the timing and placing of the practice of this new creation that we now turn.

The Ordinary Means of Hope

We have tried to shift the context for considering hope from primarily an analysis of a personal condition of the heart to primarily the dynamic and structure of that covenantal community kept hopeful throughout perennial despair and across generations and ages. This will not work, however, unless we acknowledge the ordinary means of hope.

The holiness of God's people is historically mediated holiness, accommodated holiness. It comes to us in doses and strengths we can take in different seasons and contexts of our lives. Those successive seasons and contexts are our personalized places within the *futureward*-moving band of freely forgiven sinners united to Christ by the Holy Spirit.

The texture and rhythm of this hopeful life are there whether we realize it and live by it or not. The enjoyment of, the happy participation in this benevolence is, however, not automatic: it — as Calvin says of the right knowledge of God — does not flit about in the brain but takes root in the heart. This rootage in the heart requires regular cultivation. This blessedness, this happy freedom is (to use another of Calvin's images) a planting watered by the Holy Spirit the same way a desert blooms with the coming of moisture.

Along with many lofty things which are said about spirituality, one of the essential points is a grittily earthy one. It is that the practice of Christian freedom, true piety, is a daily, ordinary, regular, habitual cadence. The joy of Christian freedom is habitual, and is the very opposite of frantic, sporadic, capricious, avoidance-motivated, religiously heroic busyness. I deliberately use "regular" to mean a ruled, a structurally portioned, freedom which is a feature of Christian abandon. There is method in Christian madness. Discipline, discipleship, is part and parcel of spontaneous amazement at the magnitude of grace. Ordinary cadence — method, rule, regular discipline — keeps the focus on the source of joy. It maintains concentration on the inflammatory beauty of holiness. It is indispensable to the holy felicity of those who, after all, are called more than others to rejoice and have more reason than others to rejoice.

Perhaps sometimes far too many voices have spoken in some parts of the Christian tradition warning ordinary saints against the dangers of unqualified happiness. And those warnings apparently are still in need of being sounded, especially when having a happy day is suggested as the proof of one's election (though the word is not remembered, much less its meaning). Yet it is so easy to get caught reacting against what Flannery O'Connor calls "eek-eek euphoria" that one can become, ironically enough, counterdependent on those who confuse giddiness with blessedness. When that happens, we need to hear a different warning. Frederick Buechner puts the matter as well as anyone when he speaks of finally giving up a rule he had laid down for himself. That rule had been

> that I had no right to be happy unless the people I loved — especially my children — were happy too. I have come to believe that that is not true. I have come to believe instead that we all of us

have not only the right to be happy no matter what but also a kind of sacred commission to be happy — in the sense of being free to breathe and move, in the sense of being able to bless our own lives, even the sad times of our lives, because through all our times we can learn and grow, and through all our times, if we keep our ears open, God speaks to us his saving word. Then by drawing on all those times we have had, we can sometimes even speak and live a saving word to the saving of others. I have come to believe that to be happy inside ourselves — to live less and less as the years go by in the dungeon of the Little Ease and more and more in the still chapel where beyond all understanding there is peace — is in the long run the best we can do both for ourselves and for the people closest to us. If we do it right, maybe they can be helped to be a little stronger through our strength, maybe even a little happier through our happiness.[10]

What are the healing practicalities of hope? The ordinary means of hope are the same as the ordinary means of grace. The only reason for this redundant phrase is to emphasize the fact that our experienced, practiced hope is response to God's freeing favor mediated historically. This means especially that the ordinary means of hope have to do with quickening, correcting, healing that particular cultic memory at the heart of a people's and a person's identity.

I have dealt with that point earlier. It suffices here to repeat: memory in this sense is far more than recall. It is the continuity of new calling to be expected in the future from God to whom all things belong. Memory in this sense is shaped by present hopes as much as the remembered past shapes the immediately disappearing present experience. Memory in this sense is the selective material of that hope designed, as it were, in the most recent past. For that is what the present is, the most instantaneously passing past, which is so brilliant that it seems to us to endure for the presently envisioned future. That is why the healing of memories

10. Frederick Buechner, *Telling Secrets: A Memoir* (San Francisco: Harper, 1991), p. 102.

is letting go a diseased past for a sane new future anticipatorily experienced in the present.

I need also here to connect again with an earlier point, namely, that God's presence is mediated presence. At one level this claim sounds so innocuous as to not even raise a fraction of an eyebrow. But this is one of those smoothed-down, user-friendly claims which in their honest angularity are scandalous; we must keep stubbing our toe on this scandal if we are to get it. The *Transcending One* freely elects to be the *Immanending One.* It is only through God's freely efficacious self-disclosure that we even can point to, much less conceive of, those encounters with the *Immanending One* through which we know we are dealt with by more than immanence. This is the point of the confession that Jesus Christ is truly God, truly human, one person. The ordinary means of grace are not duplications (!) of the incarnation, which (or rather, who) happened and happens to be rather singular! The ordinary means of grace are the ways, the means, the media, the materiality by which the Holy Spirit takes the ordinary things of this world and sets them apart for the quickening and correcting and healing of love, faith, and hope.

When the Westminster divines called the means of grace "ordinary," they did not intend to connote "unexceptional." Yes, special use is made of what is unexceptionally provided, parallel to the relation between general and special providence. However, the primary sense of "ordinary" in the case of preaching, sacraments, and prayer refers to the way they function as confirming instruments of God's saving benevolence. Through these instruments God quickens and sustains faith and continually refocuses trust on faith's proper end. A favorite word of the Westminster divines for this instrumentality was "efficacity." The means of grace are efficacious not of themselves nor of the faith of the participant; they are efficacious by virtue of the presence and activity of the God who elects to keep covenant with his people. The Word and the Spirit are never separated either in God's life as pure love or in God's life as purifying love. Preaching, sacraments, and prayer are efficacious means of grace because through the designated elements the people of God participate by grace alone through faith in the creature's spatial, timely, energetic mission of the triune God.

We have noted in the previous section that remembering the Sabbath is inseparable from doing justice. As originally conceived, the practice of the *jubilee year* was a rather remarkable application of that timing to the larger social context. It was another instance of the practicality of sanctification.

The jubilee is not an occasional outburst; it is but the regularization of what is explicitly provided as integral to the people's holiness in Leviticus. I quote the following in full from chapter 19 of Leviticus:

> When you reap the harvest of your land, you shall not reap your field to its very border, neither shall you gather the gleanings after your harvest. And you shall not strip your vineyard bare, neither shall you gather the fallen grapes of your vineyard; you shall leave them for the poor and the sojourner: I am the LORD your God.
>
> You shall not steal, nor deal falsely, nor lie to one another. And you shall not swear by my name falsely, and so profane the name of your God: I am the LORD.
>
> You shall not oppress your neighbor or rob him. The wages of a hired servant shall not remain with you all night until morning. You shall not curse the deaf or put a stumbling block before the blind, but you shall fear your God: I am the LORD.
>
> You shall do no injustice in judgment; you shall not be partial to the poor or defer to the great, but in righteousness shall you judge your neighbor. You shall not go up and down as a slanderer among your people, and you shall not stand forth against the life of your neighbor: I am the LORD.
>
> You shall not hate your brother in your heart, but you shall reason with your neighbor, lest you bear sin because of him. You shall not take vengeance or bear any grudge against the sons of your own people, but you shall love your neighbor as yourself: I am the LORD. (RSV)[11]

11. Cf. John D. Davis, "Jubilee," in *The Westminster Dictionary of the Bible,* rev. Henry Snyder Gehman (Philadelphia: Westminster, 1944), p. 333.

Practical sanctification is the right use of the goods of this world, including time and resources. Central to this practical sanctification is the vocation to be stewards, keepers in trust, of that which God freely gives for the use and delight of all God's creatures. It is true that we do not belong to ourselves but only to our Lord; and that clarity of belonging applies to other people and to their common environment. The destruction of things and people who belong not to ourselves but to God — that destruction is not just a dreadful case of mismanagement: it is sin of the most blatant form. It is real concupiscence because it is a stopping of the ears against the vocation to be what God created and redeemed us to be: instruments of God's outgoing love for his creation and derivatively agents of love for each other — and, paradoxically, agents of love for self.

There are two curiously complementary meanings of jubilee: jubilee as a period for practical repentance, and jubilee as time filled with happiness as a holy thing.

The whole of Leviticus is about getting down to specifics, but chapters 17–25 are particularly detailed. Chapter 25 enumerates the reasons for a jubilee year and its practicalities. As with any tight code, the strictest of its observants are dependent for their daily care on the services of its more generous interpreters. Leaving all the land fallow once every seven years (the units into which the forty-nine-year period is divided) would make for institutionalized hardship were it not for those who prepared granaries. Otherwise, the whole point of the jubilee would be subverted, namely, the equalization of care to all — including the care of the land and the work animals. The land and the beasts also, in effect, need the equivalent benefits of Sabbath rest. There is a planned, regular, ordinary cycle of repose, of becoming unburdened, also for them and for their beginning again refreshed.

There is the closest possible connection between jubilee as an institution for social equalization and renewal and jubilee as a time for full, complete, and plenary happiness. There are numerous wordy ways of defining that connection, but it seems congruent to refer to a song to do so: the one made popular by Mary Chapin Carpenter entitled "Jubilee." The text is set to a tune, rhythm, and skilled instrumentation which move the lame of heart to leap. The theopoiesis has its own speech. But one point cannot be mumbled: there are comfort and joy contained in the promise that those who love you will wait as long as needs be to welcome you, free for the future, under the wishing tree from which the halcyon days are now seen for what they were and are. This brings us back to the connection between holiness and happiness, and the way each defines the fullest meaning of the other. The particular happiness here is the life of walking in the light. For those of the Christian persuasion, this light has a particular and inclusive reference. Holy happiness and hilarious sanctity are the creaturely shining back, responsive refulgence, of the light to lighten the nations. That is why the ancient hymn is called *Phōs Hilaron:* there is a happy holiness of those who are moved by the beauty of the Holy Other to luminous delight.

Bibliography

Allen, Diogenes. *Philosophy for Understanding Theology.* Atlanta: John Knox, 1985.

Alston, Wallace M. *The Church.* Atlanta: John Knox, 1984.

————, ed. *Theology in the Service of the Church: Essays in Honor of Thomas W. Gillespie.* Grand Rapids: Eerdmans, 2000.

Anderson, Bernhard. *Understanding the Old Testament.* Englewood Cliffs, N.J.: Prentice-Hall, 1957.

Armstrong, Brian G. "Duplex cognitio Dei, Or? The Problem and Relation of Structure, Form, and Purpose in Calvin's Theology." In *Probing the Reformed Tradition,* edited by E. McKee and B. Armstrong, pp. 135-53. Louisville: Westminster/John Knox, 1989.

Bach, Johann Sebastian. *Passionsmusik nach dem Evangelisten Matthaeus.* Edited by Georg Schumann. London: Ernst Eulenberg, n.d. (ca. 1929).

Balke, Willem. *Calvin and the Anabaptist Radicals.* Grand Rapids: Eerdmans, 1981.

Ball, Milner S. *The Word and the Law.* Chicago: University of Chicago Press, 1993.

Balthasar, Hans Urs von. *The Christian State of Life.* San Francisco: Ignatius, 1983.

————. *Herrlichkeit: Eine Theologische Aesthetik.* 3 vols. Einsiedeln: Johannes, 1961-69.

————. *Presence and Thought: Essay on the Religious Philosophy of Gregory of Nyssa.* San Francisco: Ignatius, 1995.

————. *Truth Is Symphonic: Aspects of Christian Pluralism.* San Francisco: Ignatius, 1987.

Barth, Karl. *Church Dogmatics.* Vols. I/1–IV/1. Edinburgh: T. & T. Clark, 1936-69.

———. *The Göttingen Dogmatics: Instruction in the Christian Religion.* Vol. 1. Grand Rapids: Eerdmans, 1991.

———. *The Humanity of God.* Richmond: John Knox, 1960.

———. *Die Kirchliche Dogmatik.* Vols. I/1–IV/1. Zollikon-Zurich: Evangelisher Verlag, 1932ff.

———. *The Word of God and the Word of Man.* New York: Harper and Bros., 1957.

Battles, Ford Lewis. "God Was Accommodating Himself to Human Capacity." In *Readings in Calvin's Theology,* edited by Donald K. McKim, pp. 24-42. Grand Rapids: Baker, 1984.

Bernhardt, Reinhold, and David Willis. "Theologia Crucis." In *Evangelisches Kirchenlexikon,* edited by E. Fahlbusch et al., vol. 7, cols. 734-36. Göttingen: Vandenhoeck & Ruprecht, 1996.

Bieler, Andre. *Architecture in Worship.* Edinburgh: Oliver and Boyd, 1965.

———. *The Politics of Hope.* Grand Rapids: Eerdmans, 1974.

———. *The Social Humanism of Calvin.* Richmond: John Knox, 1964.

Bohatec, Josef. *Zur Neuesten Geschichte des Ontologischen Gottesbeweises.* Leipzig: A. Deichert, 1906.

Boisset, Jean. *Calvin et la Souveraineté de Dieu.* Paris: Seghers, 1964.

Bonhoeffer, Dietrich. *The Communion of Saints.* New York: Harper and Row, 1963.

———. *The Cost of Discipleship.* New York: Macmillan, 1965.

———. *Letters and Papers from Prison.* Enlarged edition by Eberhard Bethge. New York: Macmillan, 1972.

Botman, H. Russel. "Theology after Apartheid: Paradigms and Progress in South African Public Theologies." In *Theology in the Service of the Church: Essays in Honor of Thomas W. Gillespie,* edited by Wallace M. Alston, pp. 36-51. Grand Rapids: Eerdmans, 2000.

Bouwsma, William. *John Calvin.* New York: Oxford University Press, 1988.

Braaten, Carl, and Robert W. Jenson, eds. *Christian Dogmatics.* Vol. 1. Philadelphia: Fortress, 1984.

Brown, Peter. *Augustine of Hippo.* Berkeley: University of California Press, 1969.

Brueggemann, Walter, and Patrick D. Miller. *The Covenanted Self: Explorations in Law and Covenant.* Minneapolis: Fortress, 1999.

Buber, Martin. *I and Thou.* 2nd ed. New York: Charles Scribner's Sons, 1958.

Buechner, Frederick. *Brendan.* New York: Atheneum, 1987.

———. *Listening to Your Life.* San Francisco: Harper, 1992.

Butin, Philip. *Reformed Ecclesiology: Trinitarian Grace According to Calvin.* Princeton: Princeton Theological Seminary, 1994.

Calvin, John. *Institutes of the Christian Religion.* Edited by J. T. McNeill. Translated by F. L. Battles. 2 vols. Philadelphia: Westminster, 1960.

―――. *Institution de la Religion Chrestienne.* Edited by J.-D. Benoit. 5 vols. Paris: J. Vrin, 1957-.

―――. *Johannis Calvini Opera Selecta.* Edited by P. Barth and W. Niesel. 5 vols. Munich: Chr. Kaiser, 1926-36.

Carr, Anne E. *Transforming Grace: Christian Tradition and Women's Experience.* San Francisco: Harper, 1988.

Carter, Harold A. *The Prayer Tradition of Black People.* Valley Forge, Pa.: Judson, 1976.

Charry, Ellen. *By the Renewing of Your Minds: The Pastoral Function of Christian Doctrine.* New York: Oxford University Press, 1997.

Congar, Yves. *I Believe in the Holy Spirit.* New York: Seabury Press, 1983.

Daniélou, Jean. *Gospel Message and Hellenistic Culture.* Vol. 2. Philadelphia: Westminster, 1972.

de Gruchy, John W. *Liberating Reformed Theology.* Grand Rapids: Eerdmans, 1991.

de Journal, Rouët, ed. *Enchiridion Patristicum.* Barcelona: Herder, 1959.

Dempsey Douglass, Jane. *Women, Freedom, and Calvin.* Philadelphia: Westminster, 1985.

Dempsey Douglass, Jane, and James F. Kay, eds. *Women, Gender, and Christian Community.* Louisville: Westminster/John Knox, 1997.

de Senarclens, Jacques. *Heirs of the Reformation.* Philadelphia: Westminster, 1963.

de Vaulx, Jules. "Holy." In *Dictionary of Biblical Theology,* edited by Xavier Léon-Dufour, 2nd ed., pp. 236-39. New York: Seabury Press, 1973.

DeVries, Dawn. "The Incarnation and the Sacramental Word." In *Toward the Future of Reformed Theology,* edited by D. Willis and M. Welker, pp. 386-405. Grand Rapids: Eerdmans, 1999.

de Waal, Esther. *The Celtic Vision.* Petersham, Mass.: St. Bede's Publications, 1990.

―――. "The Cistercians." In *A Definitive History of Abbey Dore,* edited by Ron Shoesmith and Ruth Richardson, pp. 7-14. Little Logaston Woonton Almeley, Herefordshire: Logaston Press, 1997.

―――. *Living with Contradictions.* San Francisco: Harper and Row, 1989.

―――. *Seeking God: The Way of St. Benedict.* Collegeville, Minn.: Liturgical Press, 1984.

Dillenberger, Jane. *Image and Spirit in Sacred and Secular Art.* New York: Crossroad, 1990.

Dillenberger, John. *God Hidden and Revealed.* Philadelphia: Muhlenberg, 1953.

Dowey, Edward A., Jr. *A Commentary on the Confession of 1967 and an Introduction to "The Book of Confessions."* Philadelphia: Westminster, 1968.

Duff, Nancy. *Humanization and the Politics of God: The* Koinonia *Ethics of Paul Lehmann.* Grand Rapids: Eerdmans, 1992.

Eliade, Mircea. *The Sacred and the Profane.* New York: Harcourt, Brace and World, 1957.

Evans, Francis. "The Engineer Monks." In *A Definitive History of Abbey Dore,* edited by Ron Shoesmith and Ruth Richardson, pp. 139-48. Little Logaston Woonton Almeley, Herefordshire: Logaston Press, 1997.

Fairchild, Roy W. *Finding Hope Again.* San Francisco: Harper and Row, 1980.

Faulkner, Gregory. "Return to the Eucharist: The Eucharistic Ecclesiology of Alexander Schmemann's Liturgical Theology." Ph.D. Dissertation. Princeton Theological Seminary, 2001.

Florovsky, Georges. *La Sainte Eglise Universelle: Confrontation Oecuménique.* Paris: Delachaux et Niestle, 1948.

————. *Ways of Russian Theology.* Part 1. New York: Nordland, 1979.

Forde, Gerhardt O. "Luther's Theology of the Cross." In *Christian Dogmatics,* edited by C. Braaten and R. Jenson, 1:47-63. Philadelphia: Fortress, 1984.

————. *Theology Is for Proclamation.* Minneapolis: Fortress, 1990.

Frei, Hans W. *Types of Christian Theology.* New Haven: Yale University Press, 1992.

Furlong, Monica. *Christian Uncertainties.* Cambridge, Mass.: Cowley, 1982.

Ganoczy, Alexandre. *Le Jeune Calvin: Genèse et Evolution de sa Vocation Reformatrice.* Wiesbaden: Steiner, 1966.

Gerrish, Brian A. *The Old Protestantism and the New.* Chicago: University of Chicago Press, 1982.

Gillespie, Thomas W. *The First Theologians: A Study in Early Christian Prophecy.* Grand Rapids: Eerdmans, 1994.

Graham, W. Fred. *The Constructive Revolutionary: John Calvin and His Socioeconomic Impact.* Richmond: John Knox, 1971.

Green, Clifford J. *Bonhoeffer: A Theology of Sociality.* Grand Rapids: Eerdmans, 1999.

Grillmeier, Aloys. *Christ in Christian Tradition: From the Apostolic Age to Chalcedon.* New York: Sheed and Ward, 1965.

————. *Der Logos am Kreuz.* Munich, 1956.

Grillmeier, A., and H. Bacht, eds. *Das Konzil von Chalkedon.* 3 vols. Würzburg: Echter Verlag, 1951f.

Gruber, Margareta M. *Herrlichkeit in Schwachheit: Eine Auslegung der Apologie des Zweiten Korintherbriefs 2.* Würzburg: Echter Verlag, 1998.

Gunton, Colin E. *Becoming and Being: The Doctrine of God in Charles Hartshorne and Karl Barth.* New York: Oxford University Press, 1978.

Gutiérrez, Gustavo. *Essential Writings.* Minneapolis: Fortress, 1996.

Hall, John Douglas. *God and Human Suffering: An Exercise in the Theology of the Cross.* Minneapolis: Augsburg, 1986.

———. *Steward.* Grand Rapids: Eerdmans, 1990.

Hardy, E. R., ed. *Christology of the Later Fathers.* Philadelphia: Westminster, 1954.

Hays, Richard. *Moral Vision of the New Testament.* San Francisco: HarperSanFrancisco, 1996.

Hayward, Isabel Carter. *Our Passion for Justice.* New York: Pilgrim, 1984.

Hegedüs, Loránt. *A Study in the Concept of Transcendence in Contemporary German Theology.* Edinburgh: Rutherford House, 1991.

"Heilig, das Heilige." In *Lexikon für Theologie und Kirche,* vol. 4. Freiberg: Herder, 1995.

Hemmerle, Klaus. "Holy." In *Encyclopedia of Theology,* edited by Karl Rahner, p. 641. New York: Seabury Press, 1975.

Heppe, Heinrich. *Die Dogmatik der evangelisch-reformierten Kirche.* Edited by Ernst Bizer. Neukirchen: Buchhandlung des Erziehungsvereins, 1935.

———. *Reformed Dogmatics.* Grand Rapids: Baker, 1978.

Hesselink, John. *On Being Reformed.* New York: Reformed Church Press, 1988.

Hromadke, Josef L. *Impact of History on Theology.* Notre Dame, Ind.: Fides Publishers, 1970.

Hunsinger, Deborah van Deusen. *Theology and Pastoral Counseling.* Grand Rapids: Eerdmans, 1995.

Hunsinger, George. *Disruptive Grace.* Grand Rapids: Eerdmans, 2000.

———. *How to Read Karl Barth.* New York: Oxford University Press, 1991.

Hunt, George, and John T. McNeill, eds. *Calvinism and the Political Order.* Philadelphia: Westminster, 1965.

Jaeger, Werner. *Early Christianity and Greek Paideia.* Cambridge: Belknap Press of Harvard University Press, 1961.

———. *Gregor von Nyssa: Lehre vom Heiligen Geist.* Leiden: Brill, 1966.

Jenson, Robert W. *The Triune Identity.* Philadelphia: Fortress, 1982.

———, ed. *Union with Christ: The New Finnish Interpretation of Luther.* Grand Rapids: Eerdmans, 1998.

Johnson, Elizabeth A. "The Incomprehensibility of God and the Image of God Male and Female." *Theological Studies* 45, no. 3 (September 1984): 441-80.

Jüngel, Eberhard. *The Doctrine of the Trinity: God's Being Is in Becoming.* Grand Rapids: Eerdmans, 1976.

Kasper, Walter. *Faith and the Future.* New York: Crossroad, 1982.

————. *Gegenwart des Geistes: Aspekte der Pneumatologie.* Freiberg: Herder, 1973.

————. *Kirche, Ort des Geistes.* Freiburg im Breisgau: Herder, 1976.

Kay, James F. *Christus Praesens: A Reconsideration of Rudolf Bultmann's Christology.* Grand Rapids: Eerdmans, 1994.

Kelly, J. N. D. *Early Christian Doctrine.* New York: Harper and Bros., 1958.

King, Martin Luther, Jr. *Strength to Love.* Philadelphia: Fortress, 1981.

Kingdon, Robert. *Geneva and the Coming of the Wars of Religion in France, 1555-1563.* Geneva: Droz, 1956.

Klooster, Frederick H. *A Mighty Comfort: The Christian Faith according to the "Heidelberg Catechism."* Grand Rapids: CRC Publications, 1990.

Kolfhaus, W. *Christusgemeinshaft bei Johannes Calvin.* Neukirchen: Buchhandlung des Erziehungsvereins, 1939.

Krusche, Werner. *Das Wirken des Heiligen Geistes nach Calvin.* Göttingen: Vandenhoeck & Ruprecht, 1957.

Kuhn, Karl Georg, and Otto Procksch. "Hagios." In *Theological Dictionary of the New Testament,* edited by Gerhard Kittel, vol. 1. Grand Rapids: Eerdmans, 1964.

LaCugna, Catherine. *God for Us.* San Francisco: HarperSanFrancisco, 1991.

Lane, Anthony. *Calvin and Bernard of Clairvaux.* Princeton: Princeton Theological Seminary, 1996.

Lathrop, Gordon. *Holy People: A Liturgical Ecclesiology.* Minneapolis: Fortress, 1999.

————. *Holy Things: A Liturgical Theology.* Minneapolis: Fortress, 1993.

Lauber, David Edward. "Towards a Theology of Holy Saturday: Karl Barth and Hans Urs von Balthasar." Ph.D. diss., Princeton Theological Seminary, 1999.

Lazareth, William, et al., eds. *Does Chalcedon Divide or Unite? Toward Convergence in Orthodox Christology.* Geneva: World Council of Churches, 1981.

Lee, Philip J. *Against the Protestant Gnostics.* New York: Oxford University Press, 1987.

Lee, Sang Hung. *The Philosophical Theology of Jonathan Edwards.* Princeton: Princeton University Press, 1988.

Lee, Sang Hung, et al., eds. *Faithful Imagining: Essays in Honor of Richard R. Niebuhr.* Atlanta: Scholars Press, 1995.

Lehmann, Paul. *Ethics in a Christian Context.* New York: Harper and Row, 1963.

Leith, John. *Basic Christian Doctrine.* Louisville: Westminster/John Knox, 1993.

————. *An Introduction to the Reformed Tradition*. Atlanta: John Knox, 1977.

Léon-Dufour, Xavier, ed. *Dictionary of Biblical Theology*. 2nd ed. New York: Seabury Press, 1973.

Lochman, Jan Milič. *The Faith We Confess*. Philadelphia: Fortress, 1984.

Loder, James E. *The Transforming Moment*. San Francisco: Harper and Row, 1981.

Loder, James, and James Neidhardt. *The Knight's Move: The Relational Logic of the Spirit in Theology and Science*. Colorado Springs: Helmers and Howard, 1992.

Lossky, Vladimir. *In the Image and Likeness of God*. New York: St. Vladimir's Press, 1974.

MacGregor, Geddes. *Corpus Christi*. Philadelphia: Westminster, 1959.

Mauser, Ulrich W. *Gottesbild und Menschwerdung: Eine Untersuchung zur Einheit des Alten und Neuen Testaments*. Tübingen: Mohr, 1971.

McCormack, Bruce L. *For Us and Our Salvation: Incarnation and Atonement in the Reformed Tradition*. Studies in Reformed Theology and History. Princeton: Princeton Theological Seminary, 1993.

————. *Karl Barth's Critically Realistic Dialectical Theology: Its Genesis and Development, 1909-1936*. Oxford: Clarendon, 1995.

McGrath, Alister. *Iustitia Dei: A History of the Christian Doctrine of Justification*. New York: Cambridge University Press, 1998.

————. *Luther's Theology of the Cross*. Oxford: Blackwell, 1985.

McKelway, Alexander J. *The Freedom of God and Human Liberation*. London: SCM Press, 1990.

McKelway, Alexander, and David Willis, eds., *The Context of Contemporary Theology: Essays in Honor of Paul Lehmann*. Atlanta: John Knox, 1974.

McKim, Donald K., ed. *Encyclopedia of the Reformed Faith*. Louisville: Westminster/John Knox, 1992.

McNeill, John T. *The History and Character of Calvinism*. New York: Oxford University Press, 1954.

McWilliam, Joan, ed. *Augustine: From Rhetor to Theologian*. Waterloo, Ont.: Wilfrid Laurier University Press, 1992.

Meyendorff, John. *Christ in Eastern Christian Thought*. Crestwood, N.Y.: St. Vladimir's Seminary Press, 1969.

————. *St. Gregory Palamas and Orthodox Spirituality*. New York: St. Vladimir's Seminary Press, 1974.

Meyer, Harding, and Lukas Vischer, eds. *Growth in Agreement: Reports and Agreed Statements of Ecumenical Conversations on a World Level*. New York: Paulist, 1984.

169

Micks, Marianne H. *Our Search for Identity: Humanity in the Image of God.* Philadelphia: Fortress, 1982.

Migliore, Daniel. *Faith Seeking Understanding.* Grand Rapids: Eerdmans, 1991.

Miller, Patrick D. *Interpreting the Psalms.* Philadelphia: Fortress, 1986.

Minear, Paul S. *Christians and the New Creation: Genesis Motifs in the New Testament.* Louisville: Westminster/John Knox, 1994.

Moltmann, Jürgen. *The Crucified God.* New York: Harper and Row, 1974.

———. *God in Creation.* San Francisco: Harper and Row, 1985.

———. "Liberation in the Light of Hope." In *The Context of Contemporary Theology: Essays in Honor of Paul Lehmann,* edited by Alexander J. McKelway and E. David Willis, pp. 127-54. Atlanta: John Knox, 1974.

———. *Theology of Hope.* New York: Harper and Row, 1967.

Morgenstern, J. "Year of Jubilee." In *The Interpreter's Dictionary of the Bible,* edited by George A. Buttrick et al., vol. 2. Nashville: Abingdon, 1962.

Morimoto, Anri. *Jonathan Edwards and the Catholic Vision of Salvation.* University Park: Pennsylvania State University Press, 1995.

"Moscow Statement Agreed by the Anglo-Orthodox Joint Doctrinal Commission, The." 1976. London: SPCK, 1977.

Muilenburg, James. "Holiness." In *The Interpreter's Dictionary of the Bible,* edited by George A. Buttrick et al., vol. 2. Nashville: Abingdon, 1962.

———. *The Way of Israel: Biblical Faith and Ethics.* New York: Harper and Row, 1961.

Nevin, John W. *The Mystical Presence and Other Writings on the Eucharist.* Lancaster Series on the Mercersburg Theology, edited by Bard Thompson and George H. Bricker, vol. 4. Philadelphia: United Church, 1966.

Niebuhr, H. Richard. *Christ and Culture.* New York: Harper Torchlight, 1956.

———. *The Responsible Self.* New York: Harper and Row, 1963.

Niesel, Wilhelm. *The Theology of Calvin.* Philadelphia: Westminster, 1956.

Noth, Martin. "The 'Representation' of the Old Testament in Proclamation." In *Essays on Old Testament Hermeneutics,* edited by Claus Westermann and James Luther Mays, pp. 76-88. Richmond: John Knox, 1963.

Oberman, Heiko A. *Initia Calvini: The Matrix of Calvin's Reformation.* Amsterdam: Koninklijke Nederlandse Akademie van Wetenschappen, 1991.

O'Connor, Flannery. *The Habit of Being.* New York: Farrar, Straus, and Giroux, 1979.

———. *Three: "Wise Blood," "A Good Man Is Hard to Find," "The Violent Bear It Away."* New York: New American Library, 1962.

Osterhaven, M. Eugene. *The Spirit of the Reformed Tradition.* Grand Rapids: Eerdmans, 1971.

Otto, Rudolf. *The Idea of the Holy: An Inquiry into the Non-rational Factor in the*

Idea of the Divine and Its Relation to the Rational. London: Oxford University Press, 1936.

Pannenberg, Wolfhart. *The Idea of God and Human Freedom*. Philadelphia: Westminster, 1973.

Partee, Charles. "Calvin's Central Dogma Again." In *Calvin Studies III*, Papers of the 1986 Davidson Colloquium, edited by J. Leith, pp. 39-46. Richmond: Union Theological Seminary, 1986.

Pasztor, Janos Dezso. *Leonard Ragaz: Pioneer Social Theologian*. New York, 1973.

Pattison, Bonnie L. Goding. "The Concept of Poverty in Calvin's Christology and Its Influence on His Doctrine of the Christian Life and the Church." Ph.D. diss., Princeton Theological Seminary, 1997.

Pelikan, Jaroslav. *Bach among the Theologians*. Philadelphia: Fortress, 1986.

————. *The Christian Tradition*. Chicago: University of Chicago Press, 1971-89.

————. *Imago Dei: The Byzantine Apologia for Icons*. Washington, D.C.: National Gallery of Art, 1990.

Placher, William C. *The Domestication of Transcendence*. Louisville: Westminster/John Knox, 1996.

————. *Narratives of a Vulnerable God: Christ, Theology, and Scripture*. Louisville: Westminster/John Knox, 1994.

————. *Unapologetic Theology: A Christian Voice in a Pluralistic Conversation*. Louisville: Westminster/John Knox, 1989.

————. "The Vulnerability of God." In *Toward the Future of Reformed Theology*, edited by D. Willis and M. Welker. Grand Rapids: Eerdmans, 1999.

Placher, William C., and David Willis-Watkins. *Belonging to God: A Commentary on "A Brief Statement of Faith."* Louisville: Westminster/John Knox, 1992.

Plantinga, Cornelius, Jr. "Gregory of Nyssa and the Social Analogy of the Trinity." *Thomist* 43 (1986): 33-58.

————. *Trinity, Incarnation, and Atonement*. Notre Dame, Ind.: University of Notre Dame Press, 1989.

Presbyterian Church, U.S.A. *The Constitution, Part I, Book of Confessions*. Louisville: Office of the General Assembly, 1994.

Prestige, G. L. *God in Patristic Thought*. London: SPCK, 1952.

————. "*Perichoreo* and *Perichoresis* in the Fathers." *Journal of Theological Studies* 29 (1928): 242-52.

Rahner, Karl. *The Trinity*. London: Herder, 1970.

Ricoeur, Paul. *The Conflict of Interpretations: Essays in Hermeneutics*. Evanston, Ill.: Northwestern University Press, 1974.

Rigby, Cynthia L. "The Real Word Really Became Flesh: Karl Barth's Contribution to a Feminist Incarnational Christology." Ph.D. diss., Princeton Theological Seminary, 1998.

Sakenfeld, Katharine Doob. *Faithfulness in Action.* Philadelphia: Fortress, 1985.

Sauter, Gerhard. *Einführung in die Eschatologie.* Darmstadt: Wissenschaftliche Buchgesellschaft, 1995.

Smedes, Lewis B. *A Pretty Good Person.* San Francisco: Harper and Row, 1990.

Sonderegger, Katherine. *That Jesus Christ Was Born a Jew: Karl Barth's Doctrine of Israel.* University Park: Pennsylvania State University Press, 1992.

Soulen, Kendall. *The God of Israel and Christian Theology.* Minneapolis: Fortress, 1996.

Stackhouse, Max L. *Creeds, Society, and Human Rights.* Grand Rapids: Eerdmans, 1984.

Stead, Christopher. *Divine Substance.* Oxford: Clarendon, 1977.

Stringfellow, William. *Free in Obedience.* New York: Seabury Press, 1964.

Terrien, Samuel. *The Elusive Presence: The Heart of Biblical Theology.* San Francisco: Harper and Row, 1978.

Tillich, Paul. *Systematic Theology.* 3 vols. Chicago: University of Chicago Press, 1951-63.

Torrance, Thomas F. *The Christian Doctrine of God: One Being, Three Persons.* Edinburgh: T. & T. Clark, 1996.

————. *Reality and Scientific Theology.* Edinburgh: Scottish Academic Press, 1985.

————. *Royal Priesthood.* Edinburgh: Oliver and Boyd, 1955.

————. *Space, Time, and the Incarnation.* London: Oxford University Press, 1969.

————. *Space, Time, and the Resurrection.* Grand Rapids: Eerdmans, 1976.

Van Dyk, Leanne. *The Desire of Divine Love: John McLeod Campbell's Doctrine of the Atonement.* New York: P. Lang, 1995.

————. "Toward a New Typology of Reformed Doctrines of Atonement." In *Toward the Future of Reformed Theology,* edited by D. Willis and M. Welker, pp. 225-38. Grand Rapids: Eerdmans, 1999.

Volf, Miroslav. *After Our Likeness: The Church as the Image of the Trinity.* Grand Rapids: Eerdmans, 1998.

————. "Theology, Meaning and Power: A Conversation with George Lindbeck on Theology and the Nature of Christian Difference." In *The Nature of Confession,* edited by Timothy R. Phillips and Dennis L. Okholm, pp. 45-56. Downers Grove, Ill.: InterVarsity, 1996.

Wainwright, Geoffrey. *Doxology.* New York: Oxford University Press, 1980.

Wallace, Ronald S. *Calvin's Doctrine of the Word and Sacraments.* Grand Rapids: Eerdmans, 1957.

Webster, John. *Barth's Ethics of Reconciliation.* Cambridge: Cambridge University Press, 1995.

Welker, Michael. *God the Spirit.* Minneapolis: Fortress, 1994.

———. *What Happens in Holy Communion?* Grand Rapids: Eerdmans, 2000.

———, ed. *Diskussion über Jürgen Moltmanns Buch "Der Gekreuzigte Gott."* Munich: Kaiser, 1979.

Wencelius, Leon. *l'Esthétique de Calvin.* Paris: "Les Belles Lettres," 1937.

Wendel, François. *Calvin: Origins and Development of His Religious Thought.* New York: Harper and Row, 1963.

Wesley, John. *Sermons on Several Occasions.* Rev. ed. London: Epworth Press, 1946.

Westminster Dictionary of the Bible, The. Edited by John D. Davis. Revised by Henry Snyder Gehman. Philadelphia: Westminster, 1944.

Willis, David. *Calvin's Catholic Christology.* Leiden: Brill, 1966.

———. "Calvin's Use of Substantia." In *Calvinus Ecclesiae Genevensis Custos,* edited by W. Neuser, pp. 289-301. Frankfurt am Main: Lang, 1984.

———. "The Conditions of Experiential Dogmatics." *Princeton Theological Seminary Bulletin,* New Series 2, no. 3 (1979): 232-50.

———. "Extra Calvinisticum," "Finitum non capax infiniti," and "Ubiquity." In *Encyclopedia of the Reformed Faith,* edited by Donald McKim. Louisville: Westminster/John Knox, 1992.

———. "Forgiveness and Gratitude: The Doctrine of Justification in the Heidelberg Catechism." *Harvard Divinity Bulletin,* October 1963, pp. 11-24.

———. "Proclaiming Liberation for the Earth's Sake." In *For Creation's Sake,* edited by Dieter T. Hessel, pp. 55-70. Philadelphia: Geneva Press, 1985.

———. "A Reformed Doctrine of the Eucharist and Ministry and Its Implications for Roman Catholic Dialogues." *Journal of Ecumenical Studies* (spring 1981): 295-305.

———. *The Second Commandment and Church Reform: The Colloquy of St. Germain-en-Laye, 1562.* Princeton: Princeton Theological Seminary, 1994.

———. "The Steadfastness of the Holy Spirit." In *Evangelism in the Reformed Tradition,* edited by Arnold B. Lovell, pp. 85-95. Decatur, Ga.: CTS Press, 1990.

———. "The *Unio Mystica* and the Assurance of Faith according to Calvin." In *Calvin: Erbe und Auftrag* (Festschrift for W. Neuser), edited by W van't Spijker. Kampen: Kok Pharos, 1991.

———. "Women's Ordination: Can the Church Be Catholic without It?" In *Women, Gender, and Christian Community,* edited by Jane Dempsey Douglass and James F. Kay, pp. 82-91. Louisville: Westminster/John Knox, 1997.

Wilmore, Gayraud S., and James H. Cone, eds. *Black Theology: A Documentary History, 1966-1979.* Maryknoll, N.Y.: Orbis, 1979.

Wingren, Gustaf. *Man and the Incarnation: A Study of the Biblical Theology of Irenaeus.* Philadelphia: Muhlenberg, 1959.

Wolff, Hans Walter. *Anthropology of the Old Testament.* Philadelphia: Fortress, 1974.

Young, Josiah Ulysses. *No Difference in the Fare: Dietrich Bonhoeffer and the Problem of Racism.* Grand Rapids: Eerdmans, 1998.

Zimmerli, Walther. "Promise and Fulfillment." In *Essays on Old Testament Hermeneutics,* edited by Claus Westermann and James Luther Mays, pp. 89-122. Richmond: John Knox, 1963.

Zizioulas, George. *Being as Communion: Studies in Personhood and the Church.* Crestwood, N.Y.: St. Vladimir's Seminary Press, 1985.

Index

Calvin, John, 43-45, 122-24; justification and sanctification, order of treating, 57-58; uses of the law, 155; wonderful exchange, doctrine of, 155

Carpenter, Mary Chapin, 128, 161-63

Carter, Harold, 52n.18

Chain of new being, 98, 107

Chalcedon, Council of, 30-31, 75, 79, 95-96

Christ, union of believers with *(unio Christi)*, 37ff., 49-50; and assurance of faith, 39n.4; and Calvin's theology, 39-45; and *communio sanctorum*, 24ff.; hypostatic union and union with believers, 39-43; indwelling of Christ, 42n.8; mystical, 40-41; *totus Christus,* 37; "wonderful exchange," 42n.9, 50, 109

Christology: and assurance of salvation, 39; Chalcedonian, 30-32; "Christ only" and "Christ alone," 39-40, 45; the coming one, 148; communication of properties, 94, 101, 105, 109; covenant, old and new, 20-21; *Deus manifestatus in carne,* 92; eternal word, 24; *etiam calvinisticum* and *extra patristicum,* 29-32; from below and above, 14; *homoousios* and *homoiousios,* 78; hypostatic union, 30-31; Mediator of creation and redemption, 77; *status humiliationis* and *status exaltationis,* 13; suffering servant, sacrifice of, 149-50; titles of Jesus, 22, 26; *totus Christus,* 37; whole course of Christ's obedience, 43; wonderful exchange, 155. *See also Assumptio carnis;* Incarnation; Resurrection

Christocentrism, 36n.3

Church, 3, 14, 25. *See also Communio Sanctorum*

Commonweal: and beauty, 132-36; and prophetic word, 132-34; and cove-nant, 133; and right use of power, 134-35

Communio sanctorum, 20, 33ff., 49n.17, 83, 104

Conscience, 117-18, 124

Continuity and discontinuity: of crucified and risen one, 16ff.; and *creatio ex nihilo,* 16n.12, 147; old and new covenant, 20-21

Conversion: Barth's treatment of, 147; of delight, 112ff.; forgiveness and the assurance of faith, 39-40; and thanksgiving, 138n.1

Covenant: analogy and *perichoresis,* 74; and being, 72; and God's fidelity and nature, 24; old and new covenants, relation of, 9-11, 75-77

Covenantal ontology, 70-75

Creation: 90ff., 100, 108; and God's acceptation, 114. *See also* Anthropology; God, freedom of; Macrocosm and microcosm; Stewardship

Cross: and Christ's total obedience, 43; cruciform knowledge, 9-15, 112; of the risen Lord, 15ff.; *theologia crucis,* senses of and misuses of, 11-12; and theological method, 8-14, 57-58

Daniélou, Jean, 66n.10, 118n.4

Decalogue: and resurrection, 156; structure of, 152; three uses of the law, 154-55

Delight: conversion of, 112ff.; and justice, 111; use and enjoyment, 54, 121-23

de Senarclens, Jacques, 13

de Waal, Esther, 7, 113n.2, 138n.1

Duplex gratia, 53

Edwards, Jonathan, 120n.7

Election, 35

Elements: consecration of, 47